T0301812

RISK, VALUE
AND DEFAULT

World Scientific Series in Finance
(ISSN: 2010-1082)

RISK, VALUE
AND DEFAULT

Oliviero Roggi

University of Florence, Italy & New York University, USA

World Scientific

NEW JERSEY · LONDON · SINGAPORE · BEIJING · SHANGHAI · HONG KONG · TAIPEI · CHENNAI

Published by

World Scientific Publishing Co. Pte. Ltd.
5 Toh Tuck Link, Singapore 596224
USA office: 27 Warren Street, Suite 401-402, Hackensack, NJ 07601
UK office: 57 Shelton Street, Covent Garden, London WC2H 9HE

Library of Congress Cataloging-in-Publication Data
Roggi, Oliviero.
  Risk, value and default / by Prof Oliviero Roggi (University of Florence, Florence, Italy).
  pages cm. -- (World scientific series in finance, ISSN 2010-1082 ; vol. 8)
  Includes index and Bibliography.
  ISBN 978-9814641715
  1. Risk management. 2. Value. 3. Default (Finance). I. Title.
  HD61.R653 2015
  338.5--dc23
                                        2014047545

British Library Cataloguing-in-Publication Data
A catalogue record for this book is available from the British Library.

In-house Editors: Chandrima Maitra/Li Hongyan

Typeset by Stallion Press
Email: enquiries@stallionpress.com

Printed in Singapore

FOREWORD

Professor Oliviero Roggi has written an important text and scholarly/practical guide for understanding the interaction between enterprise risk management and corporate valuation. Researchers have known for a long time that risk plays an important, indeed central, role in determining the appropriate discount rate to be used in a sophisticated valuation model. In today's world, however, the very risk of survival, especially for financial institutions, is central to the health of the world's capital markets and its impact on the global economy.

Roggi has shown quite effectively, the interface between insolvency risk and enterprise risk and their joint impact on firm valuation. The importance of avoiding unexpected negative influences on firm cash flows is highlighted. I have been emphasizing the importance of measuring the insolvency risk, i.e., distress probability of companies for several decades. In Chapters 1 and 3 of this book, Professor Roggi has correctly emphasized this risk and various conceptual ways to measure it. In the following chapter, he effectively applies these concepts to the assessment of enterprise risk for firms in Italy, showing his expertise in bridging the gap between theoretical concepts and pragmatic application. As such, even without the theoretical background information provided, this book should be required reading for managers, owners, creditors and potential investors in small and medium sized enterprises.

I had the honor and privilege of participating in a conference in Firenze (June 2007), organized by Professor Roggi, on my 40 years of contributions to the area of distressed firm analytics. At this event, I observed the many aspects of enterprise risk models and management that Professor Roggi and this book advocate. It was an impressive display of works by researchers from numerous locations in the world, giving testimony to the importance and relevance of risk management. I expect that this volume will form an important part of the literature in this subject.

We need to pay more attention to risk management in the future, even for firms that are only indirectly impacted by the world's economic and financial problems. This is so for firms of all sizes even if they operate in relatively small, regional locations. This book achieves the objectives of combining sound conceptual analytics and regional firm data to suggest tangible information and guidelines for firms as well as for analysts and advisors of these entities.

Edward I. Altman
Max L. Heine Professor of Finance
NYU Stern School of Business

CONTENTS

ABOUT THE CONTRIBUTORS

Oliviero Roggi

Professor of Corporate Finance,
University of Florence and NYU Stern

Oliviero earned his PhD in Management and Finance at University of Bologna and City University Business School European Joint PhD program in 1998. He was a Visiting Researcher at the City University Business School from 1998 to 2000 and was appointed as Assistant Professor in Corporate Finance in 2000. Since 2004 he holds the post of Professor of Corporate Finance at University of Florence. Oliviero Roggi is also the founder of the Finanza Firenze Research Center, established in 2007. In 2008 he also founded, together with Edward Altman — NYU Stern Salomon Center, the International Risk Management Conference.

He also acts as a consultant at European Commission, Regione Toscana (Italy) and other public-owned entities and is doing research in the area of Enterprise Risk Management, in particular Credit Risk since 2004. Oliviero is an active member of the Scientific Committee of the Country Risk Forum of Associazione Bancaria Italiana (ABI — Italian Bankers Association). He has published papers and books on SME rating and on rating models.

He co-authored the third Italian edition of *Applied Corporate Finance* with his colleague Aswath Damodaran. Oliviero is also NYU Stern Visiting Scholar since 2009 and consultant at IFC World Bank group since 2010. Recently Prof. Roggi was appointed Visiting Research Professor at Fundaçao Gctulio Vargas in Sao Paulo (Brazil).

Alessandro Giannozzi

Assistant Professor of Corporate Finance,
Link Campus University — Rome

Alessandro earned his PhD in Finance at the University of Trieste in 2010. He was a Research Fellow at the University of Florence from 2005–2010, and has been appointed Adjunct Professor of Business Finance at Kent State University since 2011. He is Assistant Professor of Corporate Finance at Link Campus University — Rome since 2014 and also works as a consultant at Regione Toscana, Chamber of Commerce and multinational companies. Alessandro is a member of the organizing committee of the International Risk Management Conference. He has published several papers in international journals and books on SME credit rating, CoCo Bonds, corporate liquidity risk and fair value disclosure.

INTRODUCTION

The concept of risk has always been embedded in the human life. Even before Luca Pacioli set his probability puzzle, solved two centuries later by Fermat and Pascal, uncertainty and risk were affecting peoples' lives. To some extent, the society during those times was not so different from the modern era. The only relevant difference is that in today's world we have achieved partial results in understanding and managing risk and uncertainty. The results are not so encouraging and scholars are asked to develop new and better tools to predict future events and their economic consequences. Having said so, in the last 40 years finance and banking scholars have been debating about the source and nature of risk. A well-established body of knowledge is available to the scientific community, but still much more is expected in order to make this knowledge available to practitioners and corporations. In particular, I found interesting and not enough investigated, the relationship between risk generation, risk management, and corporate value from an interdisciplinary perspective. This book intends to address the problem of how corporations should deal with risk and, in doing it, how they can maximize shareholder value.

The book contains our original contribution in attempting to conceptually and empirically coordinate among these three concepts.

Since Basel II and III have been in force, risk management is a key topic in the agenda of both financial and non-financial corporations. Non-financial corporations are concerned with the supply of new finance. In doing so, they are interested in risk management as an important tool for mitigating risk and minimizing the cost of capital. On the other hand, financial institutions are forced to apply for capital adequacy requirement as enforced by the regulating authorities. The combination of the two factors gave an impetus to the research and development of models and techniques for the assessment of risk in general and financial risk in particular.

An increasing body of knowledge, dedicated to international financial reporting standards (IFRS), has helped to understand more about uncertainty and fair value estimation. This also drives to a more structured risk assessment and mitigation.

In recent years, scholars have posted several general and disagreeing definitions of risk. The perspective is that of business finance which focuses on the relation between enterprise risk, the process whereby it is identified and handled, and the value of the firm. The starting theoretical paradigm is that of the neoclassical theory of finance, whose goal is maximizing the value of the firm.

The volume is subdivided into two independent parts, which hold the five chapters that comprise the work.

Chapter 1 illustrates the main definitions and classifications of risk, linking the latter to the company's value from an economic–financial standpoint. **Chapter 2** introduces corporate risk management and illustrates concepts and processes necessary for risk analysis, quantification of a firm's capital, or venture capital, and the risks assumed by the entities that finance the firm. The logic is to guide the reader from the definitions of the first chapter to the more specific contents of the financial risk of insolvency, which will be the subject of the second part. The objective is to lead to an understanding of how enterprise risk, generated by strategic decisions, must be identified, estimated and dealt with adequate tools in order to avoid negative consequences that can diminish enterprise earnings and not allow compliance with the principle of value maximization. Risk identification, assessment, and treatment stages are discussed in detail.

In the **second part**, the author deals with the subject of the firm's financial adequacy. **Chapter 3**, introduces the concept of default risk, placing it within the context of the Basel II and III agreements and in the perspective of bankers. This chapter introduces the risk assessment models and attempts to clarify the relationship among credit risk, default, and pricing of debt for companies. It ends with a report on the impact of Basel II and III rules to corporations. Credit risk components (probability of default, loss given default, and exposure at default) and their relationship with firm's cost of debt are presented in detail.

Chapter 4 presents the results of an empirical analysis aiming to select the discriminant variables to predict the corporate default. After a brief historical review of the major techniques and methodologies used by scholars, the determining factors of the risk of default are presented, as identified through theoretical research hypotheses. This chapter also gives an account of how these variables can be measured. Selecting the discriminating variables of a predictive model across different industries involves the reader in the final part of the chapter.

The results of an empirical analysis performed on a sample of Italian firms are presented in **Chapter 5**. In this chapter, the aim is to review the methodologies utilized in estimating the corporation default. Results based on a parity sample of 300 + 300 Italian companies will show how Multivariate Discriminant Analysis (DA) and Logit Regression (LR) provide better estimation of Default Risk than Partial Least Squared Regression Discriminant Analysis (PLS-DA).

Part 1

THE CONCEPT OF RISK AND THE ENTERPRISE RISK MANAGEMENT

Chapter 1

THE CORPORATE RISK

Oliviero Roggi

Definition of Risk and Uncertainty for Business Purposes

Every corporation as decision maker is naturally subjected to uncertainty and risk of future events. To date, neither logical reasoning nor esotericism has been able to eliminate uncertainty regarding the future. Scholars and practitioners have developed sophisticated models for simulating the future, but none of them have been able to eliminate the uncertainty that is intrinsic in the human condition.

Because uncertainty and risk are the central concepts of this book, there is a need to provide logical and epistemological boundaries of the above mentioned concepts.

Currently, as we will see in this chapter, there is no consensus for a formal definition of risk that includes the complexities of the concept. As such, there is no agreement on the relationship between the concept of risk and uncertainty. Finance scholars from different schools, who are interested in the risk phenomenon, have tried to provide a general definition of risk and uncertainty.

Risk and Uncertainty Concepts at Work in Finance

At the beginning of the last century, A. H. Willet in *The Economic Theory of Risk and Insurance*, tried to give more content to the **definition of risk and uncertainty** by illustrating the relationship existing between the two concepts: *"Risk and uncertainty are objective and subjective aspects of* *apparent variability in the course of natural events"* (Willet, 1901, p. 24). Furthermore, in trying to offer a better illustration for the difference between the two concepts, he stated

> *"... It seems necessary to define risk with reference to the degree of uncertainty about the occurrence of a loss, and not with reference to the degree of probability that it will occur". Risk in this sense is the objective correlative of the subjective uncertainty. It is the uncertainty as embodied in the course of events in external world, of which subjective uncertainty is a more or less faithful interpretation"* (Willet, 1901, p. 8).

Frank Knight, in *Risk, Uncertainty and Profit*, (1921, p. 26) introduces additional elements to the distinction between risk and uncertainty.

> *"Uncertainty must be taken in a sense radically distinct from the familiar notion of risk, from which it has never been properly separated. The term "risk", as loosely used in everyday speech and in economic discussion, really covers two things which, functionally at least, in their causal relations to the phenomena of economic organization, are categorically different. The essential fact is that "risk" means, in some cases, a quantity susceptible of measurement, while at other times it is something distinctly not of this character; and there are far-reaching and crucial differences in the bearings of the phenomenon depending on which of the two is really present and operating. It will appear that a measurable uncertainty, or "risk" proper, as we shall use the term, is so far different from an unmeasurable one that it is not in effect an uncertainty at all. We shall accordingly restrict the term "uncertainty" to cases of the non-quantitative type. It is the true uncertainty and not risk, as has been argued, which forms the basis of a valid theory of profit and accounts from the divergence between actual and theoretical competition".*

Knight uses Willet's theory in which he treats the two concepts independently from each other and states the measurability of risk as opposed to the determinability of uncertainty.

Other authors, such as Archer and D'Ambrosio, echo Willet, specifying the concepts of risk as:

> *"certainty is the perfect knowledge of a future variable, risk is defined by the objective probability of a variable arising, uncertainty is, according to them, the consequence of attributing a subjective probability of an event occurring"* (D'Ambrosio and Archer, 1967).

More recently (Roggi, 2009; Gifford, 2010)[1] clarified how certainty, uncertainty and risk are applicable to business decisions in terms of the three essential characteristics of a decision:

(1) "Knowability"[2] of the environment in which the decision is made;
(2) Presence of alternatives;
(3) Orderable (ranking) alternatives.

According to Roggi (2009), **deciding under conditions of certainty** means operating under circumstances where the environment is known, there are alternatives for reaching the objective and the alternatives are orderable.

Decisions under conditions of risk are characterized by an imperfect knowledge of the environment and exhaustive identification of the alternatives. In this case, the order is determined through the attribution of a function of objective probability of the stochastic variable.

Decisions under conditions of uncertainty are recognized from their failure to satisfy the first and third characteristics, that is, neither the environment nor the order of alternatives are known. Uncertainty is a type of future event and it derives from an imperfect knowability of alternatives and inability of ordering them (Knight, 1921). In this case, for assessment, the decision makers must rely on the subjective distributions of future manifestations of the stochastic variable (see Table 1.1).

However, in the finance literature, the distinction between risk and uncertainty has been lost to the point that the two terms are often

Table 1.1: Decisions and Conditions of Certainty, Risk and Uncertainty.

Condition/Characteristics of Decisions	Environment Knowability	Presence of Alternatives	Orderability of Alternatives
Certainty	Yes	Yes	Yes
Risk	No	Yes	Yes
Uncertainty	No	Yes	No

Source: Roggi (2009).

---

[1] *International Handbook Series on Entrepreneurship* (2010).
[2] In this work, we will refer to knowability as "the capability of a decision maker to be aware of the environment faced by the organization".

used as synonyms. This confusion probably derives from the fact that
the probability function once assessed either with objective or subjective
methods, the variability is explained with the same statistical tools (sigma,
beta, standard deviation, variance, skewness, kurtosis, etc).

Risk Measurement: Sigma and Beta General Indicators

Over the years, risk measurement has acquired sophisticated models that
refer indirectly to the two general indicators described below: the sigma
factor and the beta factor.

The Sigma Factor and the Characteristics of Frequency Distribution of Corporate Earnings

The study of probability distribution allows the calculation of the first
indicator known as the **sigma factor** used for risk assessment. The **sigma
factor** (σ) **or total risk** is measured by the mean square deviation and/or
the variance. In addition, the mean, mode and median and kurtosis are
associated with this measurement in order to complete a correct reading
for the total risk.

Generally in finance, in order to describe the risk of a random variable
such as yield, it is necessary to identify three groups of summary and
characteristic indicators. These are represented by:

— Position indicators;
— Risk (or dispersion) indicators;
— Shape and symmetry indicators.

All these indicators contribute to the illustration of risk assumed by a
decision maker.

In fact, it would certainly be partial to base the decision by only
observing the position indicator: the mean for this context will be named
"expected value"[3] or "mathematical expectation".

Besides the mean, other characteristics of the frequency distribution are
needed. It will be necessary to calculate the dispersion around the mean
of the possible earnings and other characteristics mentioned in following
pages.

---

[3]The "**Expected Value**" can be defined as a weighted average of the forms assumed
by a variable, where weighing coefficients are represented by the probabilities associated
with each form.

Position indicators (measures of central tendency)

The primary indicator is represented by the **expected value**: the weighted average of the possible values assumed by the variable, where weight coefficients are represented by the probabilities associated with each value. Substantially, it corresponds to the average result that an entity would obtain by repeating to infinity the experiment involving the random variable estimated. Hence, the "expected value," known as $[E(x)]$, can be defined as the "arithmetic average of the stochastic variable".

The expected value of the stochastic variable is obtained:

$$\text{discrete } \mu_x = E(x) = \sum_{j=1}^{j=k} x_j \cdot P_j = \frac{\sum x_j}{k}, \tag{1}$$

$$\text{continuous } \mu_x = E(x) = \sum_{j=1}^{j=k} x_j \cdot \prod j. \tag{2}$$

Risk (or dispersion) indicators — sigma and variance

To evaluate yield dispersion around the mean, the concepts of variance and of standard deviation are widely utilized. In statistics, **variance** is an index of dispersion of the values of a distribution around its mean. It is indicated by the symbol σ^2 (where σ is the standard deviation).

And within the scope of descriptive statistics it is:

$$\sigma^2 = \frac{1}{n} \sum_{t=1}^{n} (x_i - \mu)^2, \tag{3}$$

where μ represents the arithmetic average of the x_i values. In the case of a stochastic variable X, variance VAR (X) is defined as:

$$\text{VAR}(X) = E[(X - E[X])^2] = E[X^2 - E[X]^2]. \tag{4}$$

Beside pure statistical measures, the insurance and banking industries have developed their own specific tools.

The concept of **expected maximum loss (EML)** has become popular within the scope of risk analysis of a single project and/or an asset portfolio. This measurement estimates the negative effects of divergences from the mean value. It can be defined as the maximum level of loss with the sole exclusion of absolutely exceptional scenarios (Alexander, 1998). This is an assessment of the EML probability, while imposing a certain degree of confidence (normally 1% or 5%).

In comparison to the mean square deviation, which is an indicator of overall risk, there is a significant difference. EML tends to measure only threats and not opportunities offered by the variability of future events. This means that "EML" refers only to the so-called *downside risk*. A further element of differentiation between the two indicators is represented by the fact that the mean square deviation can be calculated both in the presence of discrete and continuous random variables, while maximum probable loss can be estimated only in the presence of continuous functions. Next to EML, it is also possible to measure an extreme scenario. In that case, EML will be measured and corresponds to the loss occurring in the worst case scenario presented by the analyst. This scenario has infinitesimal probabilities of becoming true (for instance, in the "worst case scenario" for a firm, α would have a 0.00001% probability of becoming true).

Shape and symmetry indicators

Next to variance, square deviation and maximum possible loss, it is necessary to observe the values of frequency distribution.

An initial tool is the calculation of **kurtosis**. Kurtosis is a measure of the concentration of a distribution around its mean. It measures the departure from the normal distribution, where greater flattening (platykurtic distribution) or greater peakedness (leptokurtic distribution) occurs. The most popular kurtosis measurement is the Fisher index obtained by computing the ratio between the fourth order central moment and the square of the variance. The value of the index that corresponds to normal (Gaussian) distribution is 3. A value of less than 3 indicates a platykurtic distribution, whereas a value greater than 3 indicates a leptokurtic distribution.

In finance, and specifically in risk assessment, this indicator allows a correct evaluation of deviations from the mean. High kurtosis values indicate a greater dimension of the distribution's tails. This circumstance determines a greater risk due to higher probability of extreme events.

Another useful concept in this group is the *skewness*, that is, an indicator which illustrates the prevalence of negative scenarios (negative skewness) or positive scenarios (positive skewness) in the dispersion of the values. Qualitatively, a negative skew indicates that the *tail* on the left side of the probability density function is *longer* than the right side and the bulk of the values (possibly including the median) lie to the right of the mean. A positive skew indicates that the *tail* on the right side is *longer* than the left side and the bulk of the values lie to the left of the mean.

Distribution tends to be positive values (positive skewness), when the median is lower than the mean. In this case, certain particularly high observed values will move the average toward the right. From a financial standpoint, positive skewness shows the greater probability of obtaining particularly high yields.

***

The analysis of the yield frequency distribution of an asset with all the above tools provides the most detailed assessment of risk.

The variation of earnings close to the average does not have the same effect on a firm. Only deviations that occur on the left side of the distribution, that is, the ones normally formed in scenarios with earnings lower than expected value, constitute a problem for the firm because actual yields are lower than those expected. Risk managers handle these risks, called downside risk, with care because they lead the company to reducing profits and therefore, future expectations on the firm itself.

Risk management scholars have separated risks into two groups in order to distinguish the risks of loss from the opportunity of obtaining a higher yield than expected. Pure risks may manifest actual return lower than expected, whereas speculative risks may generate return higher or lower than expected.

The Beta Coefficient

The second tool used in the assessment of risk is the **Beta** coefficient or factor.

Beta is a general tool in the study of variability induced by a phenomenon on a dependent variable. This ratio expresses the relative variability of the yield of a specific asset induced by the variation of market yields.

Finance scholars and practitioners are widely using this tool to estimate risk of assets when compared with the market variance. The beta can be used as a relative risk measure of company earnings. Other beta factors can be computed using the change in the commodity index. **The Beta**

factor is the ratio between covariance of the asset return (yield) toward the yield variance in the market portfolio. Statistically, it can be written as follows:

$$E(Ri) = Rf + \beta(R_m - R_f).$$

This ratio is used in the *Capital Asset Pricing Model* (CAPM) (Treynor, 1961; Sharpe, 1964; Lintner, 1965) for defining the risk–reward ratio.

The Beta measures the part of the asset's statistical variance that cannot be diversified from the portfolio made up of many risky assets, because of the correlation of its returns with the returns of the other assets that are in the portfolio.

Beta can be used to study the effect of variation of exogenous or endogenous variables on the firm's fundamentals such as: operating income, net income, operating cash flow, *Free Cash Flow to Equity* (FCFE), *Free Cash Flow to Firm* (FCFF) or the stock price.

Risk yield models that use multivariate analyses employ multiple Beta factors, one for each regressor. For instance, *Arbitrage Pricing Theory* (APT) (Ross, 1976) studies the fluctuation of the stock yield observing the changes of a group of macro risk factors impacting the company's earnings. These factors are considered the most significant "factors" according to the *Principal Component Analysis* (PCA).

These factorial models can be used to isolate the variability of the expected yield of a security induced by exogenous variables, such as the price of oil, the general wholesale prices index, retail prices, or other exogenous variables responsible for the market risk.

In the case of APT, after conducting a PCA whereby regressors are identified, and the subsequent multiple regression for linking the latter to the stochastic variable $E(X)$, the following formula is obtained:

$$E(X) = a + \beta_1 F_1 + \beta_2 F_2 + \beta_3 F_3 + \cdots + \beta_n F_n + \varepsilon, \qquad (5)$$

where F is from 1 to N and represents the factors determined with PCA.

$$\begin{aligned} E(X) = {} & R_f + \beta_1(E[R]_1 - R_f) \\ & + \beta_2(E[R]_2 - R_f) + \cdots + \beta_n(E[R]n - R_f) + \varepsilon, \qquad (6) \end{aligned}$$

from which the expected yield with Asset Pricing Model (APM) is obtained as a generalization of CAPM.

In the case of multifactorial models with *a priori* indication of regressors, the equation is presented as follows:

$$E(X) = a + \beta_1 V_1 + \beta_2 V_2 + \beta_3 V_3 + \cdots + \beta_n V_n + \varepsilon, \qquad (7)$$

where V is from 1 to N and represents the macroeconomic risk factors. This technique is used mainly in risk analysis because it allows an assessment of the effect on a firm's profitability caused by variations by the indicators. This allows easier interpretation of the results and directs management with more clarity with its investment and dividend choices.

Enterprise Definition and Risk

Enterprise, from the Latin *impresum* (past participle of *imprendere)*, means "taking upon oneself," indicating the act of carrying out actions and deeds capable of attaining a preset objective.

In the late 19th century, the concept of entrepreneur was present in the studies by Mill (1848) and Walras (1874).[4] The enterprise concept is also found in the work of Knight (1921), where he links the concept of uncertainty to the enterprise as a tool for the organization of the economic system. In fact, Knight states:

> "It is this true uncertainty which, by preventing the theoretically perfect outworking of the tendencies of competition, gives the characteristic form of "enterprise" to economic organization as a whole and accounts for the peculiar income of the entrepreneur" Knight (1921).

An early Italian precursor of managerial science, Zappa defined the salient characteristics of the relationship between the firm and the enterprise as an "ongoing economic entity instituted and managed for the satisfaction of human needs" (Zappa, 1927, p. 30). Later, Ceccherelli refers to the firm as a "productive entity subject to risks and variabilities of the economic environment form from its perennially perturbed system" (Ceccherelli, 1948, p. 64).

However, from the diversity of definitions, a first common element emerges of the purpose for which the entrepreneur gives rise to the enterprise through the creation and the financial management of the firm. This objective is the **satisfaction of individuals' needs**. The above-mentioned objective can be attained only if the entrepreneur

---

[4]See Mill (1848); Walras (1874).

and the enterprise equip itself, "*par anticipation*", with productive factors and organize the factors in space/temporal transformation processes that can satisfy needs by supplying goods and services.

Under this circumstance, the entrepreneur is obligated to anticipate the needs perceived by consumers. This is understood from the second common element of the definitions quoted this far. Thus, a prevailing element in the manufacturing enterprise is **the risk incurred by the entrepreneur in organizing production**.

As a risk taking entity, the enterprise is for profit, this to justify the risk retained by the entrepreneur in satisfying other people needs. The entrepreneur has the right to appropriate the profit generated by the business, which is later distributed among the shareholders or held within the enterprise to finance its expansion.

The enterprise, in this perspective, becomes a center of **economic–technical functions** (Ceccherelli, 1964; Fazzi, 1982) of manufacturing, transformation of goods, adapting to customers' requirements, and production of services and ultimately it **produces financial cash flow to equity**.

Moving to a more recent financial perspective of the firm (Damodaran, 2006),[5] the focus shifts much more on the investments and financing needed to run the business. But even in this perspective the enterprise and the risk generated are inseparable concepts. Hence, there is no enterprise without risk. This relationship can only be violated by certain enterprises such as those of disbursement. In these enterprises, the corporate form is selected as a useful tool for dispensing services to the community and it does not imply risks for the operator.

Enterprise Risks: A Classification by Nature

The nature of the risks incurred by the enterprise varies; to classify risks by nature and genesis, we can refer to some mixed literature (Crouhy, Galai and Mark, 2000; Shimpi, 2001; Hull, 2012), which distinguishes risks

---

[5]From this standpoint, the enterprise may be understood as a body characterized by investments made and by financings. In particular, it is identified as:

— The sum of investment projects which it needs to carry out its activities of production of goods and services;

— The sum of financings necessary for covering the financial requirements deriving from investments.

as follows:

— **Operating**
  ○ Operating and verification
  ○ Business risk

— **Financial**
  ○ Internal
    ▪ Insolvency
    ▪ Counterparty
    ▪ Capital structure planning
  ○ External
    ▪ Interest rate
    ▪ Currency exchange rate
    ▪ Inflation

— **Market**

Each of these can be broken down into homogeneous sub-categories and certain types of enterprises generate risks, which can be classified into more than one group.

Operating Risks

Operating risks are the deviations from expected earnings which occur as a result of carrying out the enterprise's operating activities. Because of their nature, these types of risks emerge from the decisions on the use of resources and therefore pertain to the enterprise's investment decisions. For this reason, they affect the cash flow, and the application of funds section of the *Funds Flow Statement* (FFS) in the financial report, mainly on the left side of the sources/investments statement, specifically the one on investments.

Operating risks are **verification risks**: errors, omissions, erroneous valuation. Risks such as procedural verification errors, unexpected reductions of sales prices and theft of goods owned by the enterprise, such as money, may also occur. Furthermore, the enterprise may be subject to operating risks pertaining to governance or accounting. An example of a governance risk is corporate paralysis triggered by conflicts among groups of shareholders and/or members of the board of directors. Risks pertaining to accounting originate from poor application of financial statement policies and accounting standards especially from choices about compliance with international accounting principles (US GAAP *vs.* IFRS).

Another category of operating risks is that of **employee relations**. Losses may originate from personnel management procedures, legal and class actions, exacerbation of labor disputes, loss of human resources and strategic skills held by personnel.

Increasingly more are the risks a firm incurs in organizing its **information systems**. All companies in fact do rely more and more on an IT infrastructure to run any type of business. There may be problems in synchronizing the computer infrastructure for accuracy in the flow of information and the inability to recover damage to memories. Furthermore, risks can come from third-party entities entrusted with outsourced services. These risks arise from internet use in operating a business: risks of fraud, improper use of computer infrastructures; and the so-called "bottleneck" risks and involuntary information leaks.

There is also a second **operating risks** sub group called **business risks**. This group includes risks linked to how activity is carried out and how investments are made. These are considered **business event risks**, such as: technical obsolescence risk, changes in the regulatory setup, damage to image and service interruption. The magnitude of the damage caused by the occurrence of such events depends on the industry in which the company is operating. (For instance, regulatory risk for a colossus such as *Microsoft* is much greater than that of a small software firm operating in the suburbs and producing accounting software for local firms.) Development and product supply risks (*product risks*) are generally included in operating risks, at least for deviations from forecasts, which arise because of unforeseen problems in the development and engineering of the product, warehouse management and also packaging and distribution. The enterprise also becomes subject to operating risks when it does not correctly forecast the behavior of its major competitors. This has a direct impact on product sales prices and on the market share, which in turn negatively influence the actual earnings. The difference between the realized and expected earnings can trigger financial risks such as credit lines crunch.

Among these operating risks, negative events associated with **partnership and alliance relations** may occur. For instance, the concentration of suppliers or customers, together with an imprudent management of strategic alliances or erroneous identification of third parties to whom to entrust outsourced services, may compromise the service rendered and, therefore, the expected cash flow. Furthermore, under the umbrella of business risks we can locate the so-called **legal risks**. These are mainly attributed to the conduct of top executives and board members of the enterprise.

Also included in this risk sub-category are contractual risks and the so-called **counterparty risks**. These are incurred as a consequence of granting credit to customers and suppliers. Such risks are mainly present in financial institutions where the counterpart risk is regulated by Basel III and/or similar acts.

Financial Risks (Market Risks)

Financial or market risks constitute the second group of risks incurred by the enterprise. They are identifiable as deviations from expected earnings as a result of changes in market financial variables.[6] Therefore, all potential deviations that occur are due to financing decisions. Within this group, internal risks such as insolvency, counterparty, capital structure policy risks, can be separated from external risks. External risks originate from events beyond management control, but alter the company's stock value or generate unexpected outflows. Exchange rate risks (if the financial source is expressed in foreign currency) are examples of interest and inflation risks.

Among internal **financial risks** we find the **risk of default (insolvency)**. It arises when an enterprise is unable to meet its ordinary means of payment requirements, requirements that arise during the life cycle of the enterprise. This risk is linked to the organic relationship between investments made and financial sources provided. An enterprise must operate by the financial equilibrium principle in which the equilibrium has to be verified constantly to allow the enterprise's survival. The adequacy of the **capital structure** is therefore a relevant factor in determining the insolvency risk. This adequacy is defined both in terms of the investments/sources ratio and the alternative sources of financing (financial leverage ratio).

Liquidity risk is different even if it is often confused with solvency risk. It arises when a company presents a high variability of its cash flow. This may make controlling available liquidity difficult, if not impossible. In this case, risk is presented in the form of a cash deficit, which requires an unscheduled disinvestment of assets or the negotiation of an overdraft. This ends up impacting earnings and, therefore, enterprise value.

---

[6]Merna and Al-Thani (2011).

Specifically, risk is high when an enterprise's current assets consist of assets that cannot be readily liquidated to meet payment requirements.

Another type of **financial risk** is that associated with **settlement of transactions**. Although there is no wish to suspend or not make payments pertaining to operating activities, it may happen that the geographical or organizational distance of operators causes insolvency to arise from the settlement.

Foreign exchange and interest rate risks are other exogenous financial risks. Foreign exchange risk arises when the exchange ratio between two national currencies is substantially modified. This occurrence can modify cash flow generated by various investment projects and arises in the presence of multinational business entities. This specific financial risk is relevant when the enterprise manufactures and sells in two or more markets characterized by different currencies. The unexpected increase or decrease in the value of a currency can generate significant deviations in regard to expected cash flow. Foreign exchange rate risk is two-fold in nature: it is mainly an operating risk when deviations pertain to lower proceeds from earnings in other countries or greater supply costs or other activities associated with operating management. The risk has an exquisitely financial nature when the deviation is caused by variations in the face value or principal repayment on foreign currency loans.[7]

Another source of financial risk to which enterprises are subjected to the **interest rate risk**. This concept defines deviations in the stock values and earning flows generated by an unexpected change of the interest rate in force in the capital markets. This arises due to causes beyond the control of the enterprise; external conditions lead to substantial modifications in the cost of capital. Specifically, restrictive or permissive currency policies play a determining role in the selection of which interest rate to apply.

Market Risks

The third group of risks, or **market risks**, is linked to factors exogenous to the enterprise not attributable to the financing policy. These risks are

---

[7]A well-known case of financial risk associated with foreign exchange is the one faced by hundreds of Italian families and companies when, because of particular market conditions, it was particularly advantageous to access loans in Swiss francs. The increase in value of the latter currency led to risk situations that were altogether unbearable, so that the government had to step in and arrange provisions for conversion and consolidation of risky foreign loans.

generated by a fluctuation in the market value of assets. In the literature, these events are called **position risks**. These risks often occur in enterprises with enhanced financial activity, such as financial institutions, asset management corporations, and any other enterprise with a corporate objective consisting of assets and liabilities management. In certain cases, the market risk arises due to commodities such as gold and precious metals. An unexpected fluctuation in market prices can generate the necessary devaluation of the asset with negative consequences on enterprise earnings.

∗ ∗ ∗

The above review does not pretend to be exhaustive; it can be used, however, for the purposes of an initial organization and classification of the risks an enterprise may face. However, it is inadequate when willing to study in greater depth the issue of the link between financial decisions, risk, and enterprise value. In fact, to shed light on the relationship existing among these entities it is necessary to reread the risks preciously described and attempt to link them to the investment or financing decisions.

In the next paragraph, we will learn to distinguish business from leverage risk and understand how it is shared among enterprise lenders.

Enterprise Risks: Business and Leverage Risk[8]

The analysis of risk can be conducted from the viewpoint of the enterprise. In this new perspective, risks can be classified into two homogeneous categories:

(1) **Business risk**, which is the variability of earnings as a consequence of investment acts.
(2) **Leverage risk**, measured by the variability of earnings following the enterprise's financing decisions.

The sum of the two components, total risk, is embedded in the enterprise since origination and constitutes the main motivation for investors to demand a yield.

By applying the neoclassical theory of finance it is possible to state that an enterprise is in a neutral position with regard to risks retained during operations. As such, the total risk (*asset risk*) is transferred to the

---

[8]For an in-depth analysis, see Monahan (2008).

suppliers of finance. The systematic risk is retained by the enterprise, even when the investors are diversified.

By observing the risk generated in enterprise activities before it is passed to the supplier of finance, it is possible to analyze the origin of enterprise risk.

Total enterprise risk (*asset risk*) can be broken down into business and leverage risks. These two types of risks do not have the same characteristics because business risk is ingrained in the existence of the enterprise whereas leverage risk is a probable risk that arise from the financing decisions. As a consequence of its activity, each enterprise needing investments is subject to business risk. The same cannot be said for leverage risk, which emerges significantly when the enterprise uses debt and others financial liabilities. The entrepreneur can avoid bearing this risk by not assuming debt, or limiting its size, by designing a capital structure adequate to ensure solvency and sustainability. In the "textbook case", in which the company is financing its investment by using his own resource (equity) the earnings will be subject only to the hazard derived from operating risks generated by investments. Consequently, the asset risk would be equal to the business risk and the enterprise value (V_{assets}) equal to that for the shareholders (V_{equity}).

$$\text{Total Risk} = \text{Asset Risk} = \text{Business Risk}.$$
$$V_{assets} = V_{equity}.$$

A capital structure built entirely from equity is rare and most often confined to the M & M assumptions (Modigliani and Miller, 1958, 1963; Miller, 1977). In most cases, enterprises meet their financial requirements from equity and partly from debt. In this case, next to the business risk described above, is the variability of earnings derived from financing. This variability is defined as leverage risk.

In the presence of leverage risk and in the absence of arbitrage positions (Modigliani and Miller, 1958; Miller, 1977), total risk therefore comprises business and leverage risks. Together, these are retained by the suppliers of finance in accordance to the seniority. Residual claimers are the first of all the shareholders who will bear the business risk and leverage risk generated by the capital structure decisions.

$$\text{Total Risk} = \text{Business Risk} + \text{Leverage Risk}.$$

In order to determine the asset value of the enterprise it can be concluded that it is the sum of $V_{equity} + V_{debts}$. This parity is not verified mainly because of the tax deductibility of interest expenses that increase the total value of the firm by the tax benefits (Myers, 1984).

The introduction of debt to an enterprise leads to the emergence of default risk and consequent bankruptcy costs. To calculate the value of the leveraged enterprise it is necessary to revisit the "textbook case" described above of an unleveraged enterprise to apply the appropriate correction to take into account the presence of debt.

Myers (1984) presents the calculation of the value of a leveraged enterprise as follows:

$$V_{\text{leveraged}} = V_{\text{unleveraged}} + \text{TB} - \text{BC},$$

where the value of the leveraged enterprise ($V_{\text{leveraged}}$) is the arithmetic sum of the value of the unleveraged enterprise ($V_{\text{unleveraged}}$), tax benefits associated with debt (TB) and expected direct and indirect bankruptcy costs (BC). The total enterprise value can substantially increase as the debt increases until the marginal benefit of the debt equals the marginal cost of bankruptcy.

In the case of an unleveraged firm, the Beta will be equal to the Beta of equity in the absence of debt ($\beta_{\text{equity0,100}}$), also called Unleveraged Beta ($\beta_{\text{unleveraged}}$).

In this case,

$$\beta_{\text{assets}} = \beta_{\text{equity0,100}} = \beta_{\text{unleveraged}}.$$

In the case of debt, the Beta assets measure the enterprise risk, which is the weighted average of the Betas of the various sources.

Expressing this same ratio, Beta as a measurement of enterprise risk can be stated as follows:

$$\beta_{\text{assets}} = \beta_{\text{equity}} + \beta_{\text{debts}} = \beta_e \frac{E}{E+D} + \beta_d \frac{D}{D+E}, \tag{8}$$

where β_{equity} will be Beta leveraged, that is, an indicator of the risk for a shareholder of a leveraged company and β_{debts} will be the measurement of the risk of debt holders.

In case of a solvent enterprise, the β_{debts} is equal to zero because its debt returns and market returns are uncorrelated. In this circumstance, business and leverage risks are both retained by the shareholder. In the case of insolvency, there will be a transfer of part of the risk from the shareholder to the creditor, measured by an increase in beta debts. This occurs when the enterprise's financing policies are not coherent with its investment policies, and imbalances of the financial structure arise.

In conclusion, business risk and leverage risk do not share the same characteristics and the same treatment techniques.

Business risk is inherent in enterprise activities and can be reduced by drawing on investment portfolio diversification policies. Leverage risk is an accessory risk derived from decisions regarding investment coverage and exogenous conditions that may change the cost of capital.

It is difficult to determine a correspondence between business risk and equity risk on one hand and leverage risk and debts risk on the other because both are retained by the shareholder as far as the equity is adequate to sustain the maximum expected loss. Otherwise, the emergence of insolvency risk causes one portion of both the business risk and the broader leverage risk to fall into the borrowers' hands.

Adequacy of Sources and Financial Structure Risk

The importance of an adequate financing policy is supported by the theoretical analysis of the Italian School, which contributed to the debate by developing the relationship between investment coverage and financial structure risk (Cattaneo, 1976; Pivato, 1983; Fanni, 2000).

As a result, studies on capital assets and cash (Brugger, 1980; Cattaneo, 1976), indicators of leverage and coverage of fixed assets and those of liquidity were developed.

Among the tools developed in that period is the FFS sources–investments outline. The FFS shows how changes in balance sheet accounts and income affect cash and cash equivalents, and breaks the analysis down to operating, investing, and financing activities. This document is necessary for evaluating the adequacy of sources in regard to investments.

Financing must be selected from the available sources according to the **adequacy principle**. Three types of sources for adequacy investments are identified:

(a) Horizontal;
(b) Vertical;
(c) Economic.

Horizontal adequacy occurs when sources are homogeneous by nature and by maturity with investments they finance. A measurement of horizontal adequacy is that of "capital assets" which has been largely used for in the literature. However, this measurement has the limitation of calculating adequacy by using absolute values and therefore it cannot capture the coverage margin. Because of this it is customary to use the fixed asset coverage ratio which constitutes the equivalent in the form of ratio of said capital assets. The other margin used to evaluate horizontal adequacy is the "cash margin", which is calculated by subtracting short term financial and commercial liabilities from the liquidity entries under assets. This margin has a version in the form of the *acid ratio*, one of the liquidity indicators most frequently used in the literature together with *current ratio* and *quick ratio*.

Horizontal adequacy averts insolvency and makes it possible for the enterprise to achieve financial equilibrium.

Vertical adequacy stresses proportions regarding financing sources and it can report imbalance situations in the form of excessive indebtedness compared to net assets. Equity composition ratios D/(D+E) and E/(D+E) or the well-known financial leverage ratio (D/E) can be used to measure vertical adequacy.

Financial leverage reports how many times the debt exceeds the equity.

The economic adequacy (capital adequacy) of the capital structure (financing) is met when a company in its daily operations can generate sufficient cash flows for serving the interest and debt repayments (debt service) that is generated by the liabilities. Debt does not generate financial imbalance by itself. Inadequacy occurs only when the company's operating profit after deduction of taxes is not sufficient to cover interest expenses originated by the debt itself. In other words, when the earnings before interest and taxes, EBIT $(1 - t_c)$ < interest expenses. In this case, not only is the entire operating profit absorbed by the debt service, but also a portion of these costs constitutes losses that erode the enterprise's net assets. If this situation continues over time, the enterprise is bound toward a structural imbalance and a state of distress and pre-bankruptcy takes over.

The calculation of the capacity of cash flow to service debt is measured by a series of ratios.

The first ratio between the earnings before interest, taxes, depreciation, and amortization (EBITDA) and the interest expenses is largely used in financial accounting and can be written as:

$$Interest\ Coverage\ Ratio = \frac{\textbf{EBITDA}}{interest\ expenses},$$

which compares operating income before depreciation, amortization, with interest expenses. This index does not take into account the principal repayment that should be added to the interest expenses. For this reason, practitioners use the _Debt Service Coverage Ratio_ (DSCR): Where the denominator (_Total Debt Service_) includes both the abovementioned items:

$$\mathrm{DSCR} = \frac{\mathrm{EBIT}}{total\ debt\ service}.$$

or one of its financial variants with its numerator as the FCFF:

$$\mathrm{DSCR_{Fin}} = \frac{\mathrm{FCFF}}{total\ debt\ service}.$$

If the ratio value is less than one, the company cash flow generated by operating activities is unable to serve the debt. This circumstance does bring immediately to the default because management theoretically can find new resources to issue new equity or debt. Debt coverage is a necessary condition for the survival of the enterprise in the long term.

Insolvency could always arise due to a mismanagement of the cash balance. In fact, even if the DSCR is optimal or greater than one, the company may incur an unexpected shortage of cash.

Risk and Life Cycle Stages of an Enterprise

Risk originates from uncertainty embedded in the investments and may arise differently according to the stages of life cycle in which the enterprise is. Drawing the ideal path for an enterprise involving every development stage right from the inception of a business idea to a complex enterprise, the relationship between investments, financing and typical risk, is illustrated in the following paragraphs.

The **start-up stage** is the one in which the entrepreneur formalizes the business idea and finalizes the initial organization, strategy and corporate governance. At this stage, the pioneer entrepreneur must select initial investments to start his activity and raise financial sources, mainly from his own assets, through contributions. The first financing step for an enterprise is contribution of the initial equity which is normally followed by the negotiation of new debt: mainly in the form of short-term bank debt and bank loans. In this initial development stage the production is started. Because of the newness, operating risks regarding material used, manufacturing process and distribution channel organization occur more often in this phase than in later stages. For this reason, coverage of initial investments is mainly carried out through equity and only for the portion pertaining to equipment and structures is debt resorted to. At this stage, the composition of sources is initially skewed toward equity, whereas the D/E ratio increases rapidly upon underwriting of bank debt, whether short, or medium or long term.

The next stage is **enterprise expansion**. Its objective is consolidation of activities, market share growth and broadening distribution channels beyond domestic borders. Typical investments for this stage are those pertaining to market share growth, establishment of trademarks and patents that provide competitive advantage, and expansion of net working capital due to the expansion of the distribution channels. Operating risks for logistics increase including those on sales estimates, which are of lower quality, because of the large variance caused by growth. Present for the first time are risks on international activities of the enterprise, identifiable both in foreign exchange rate and interest rate risks, which are risks of a financial nature. If the enterprise takes the path of external growth, investments will be of a prevailingly financial nature and pertains to acquisitions of equity investments in companies operating in the same or related sectors. The financial requirement at this stage is very high and must be covered by injections of new equity that can expand the debt. It is at this stage that the entrepreneur is joined by operators specialized in venture capital that can underwrite, partially or wholly, the increase in capital necessary for the expansion stage. Following this operation, the D/E ratio undergoes a reorganization allowing the enterprise to find additional sources of financing from banking institutions from which a return to higher D/E levels is obtained. From the standpoint of the financial structure, this stage is characterized by a widespread growth of debt and equity components but is inclined more in favor of debt. In fact, with debt it is possible to finance leverage and buy-out operations. In certain cases, debt service is difficult and the enterprise suffers from limited financial flexibility derived from high costs associated with debt. Furthermore, the presence of a merger and acquisition operation results in an increase in operating risk between enterprise target and bidder. This results in an increase in expectations in terms of the expected yield, which will have to adapt to the new and higher levels of risk, both financial and operating.

The stage following the enterprise expansion stage is that of **"going public"**.[9] At this stage, the management has the objective of continuing activity development in overcoming the constraints of private financial resources found in non-regulated markets. Other possible objectives (Arosio, Giudici and Paleari, 2000) that regulate this stage are:

> Disinvestment on the part of certain charter shareholders (pioneers or private bankers) of equity investments in the enterprise. This gives rise to management buy-out or family buy-out operations;
>
> An improvement in the corporate image following greater transparency necessary for accessing negotiations and also the consequence of the quantity and quality of information exchanged on the company, that is the capacity of attracting better human resources.

At this stage, the enterprise continues on its path of growth, whether internal or external, increasing the volume of its fixed assets and, in particular, investments in tangible fixed assets or financial assets (in the case of external growth through acquisitions). The huge investments necessary at this stage lead to the emergence of financial requirements of sizable dimensions which must find a temporary satisfaction in the sources of debt such as: secondary debt (*second lien*) and mezzanine financing. These sources allow the enterprise to continue with its development plans ensuring that the resources for investing is functional, strategic, and the financial reorganization process will enable the company to be listed on regulated markets. The risk generated by the enterprise is mainly caused by the difficulty in integrating the enterprise's newly acquired assets and the failure to achieve sales and profitability objectives. This is a result of the financial structure risk, which is triggered by the drawing of capital from the third-party. It is this last component of financial risk that is only partly mitigated by the enterprise by forms of financing with variable compensation, defined as semi-equity tools. An example is the underwriting of part of the enterprise profit participation loans or mezzanine loans allocated to listing operations. The D/E ratio undergoes a rapid increase which results in the injection of new capital during the Initial Public Offering stage.

---

[9]The term *"going public"* indicates the operation of the first listing of a company on a regulated market. For an in-depth analysis of the subject of value in a listing stage, see Roggi (2003).

Once the listing occurs with the help of advisors and the global coordinator (Roggi, 2003; Arosio, Giudici and Paleari, 2000), the enterprise, by this time a **"public company"**, directs its investment and financing activities taking into due consideration its relationship with the market where its stock is being traded. Investment projects are not selected on the basis of the principle of creating value, but rather pursuing the specific principle of maximizing available value for shareholders. In fact, maximizing the price of the stock replaces the value of creation objective and results in modification of investments and financing choices. On its growth path, the enterprise collects the capital issued during the IPO thus rebalancing the D/E ratio that had grown from the previous stages. In view of the high costs of listing, the enterprise will raise capital from the market, which is necessary to finance the permanent requirements highlighted at the industrial level. This occurs in the first post-listing stage in which there is a significant reduction of the D/E index. Subsequent to the listing, the enterprise will continue to expand its activity to manufacture other goods and services, or it will decide to brave the international market. In both the cases, the enterprise will benefit from a reduction of specific risk associated with its core business and will subject its investors to a mitigated risk, which is equal to systematic risk. In the literature there is no consensus on the usefulness of diversification operations undertaken by the enterprise after the listing. In fact, one line of thought (Myers, 1968; Shall, 1972) states that diversification of specific enterprise risks can be reached with smaller costs and greater ease by the investor (an individual), who may build a stock portfolio representing enterprises with diversified activities. These authors conclude that growth activities in sectors are contiguous to the one carried out and should be disincentivated and should not be the subject of post-listing growth. Other scholars, convinced of the usefulness of the enterprise as an intermediary between the needs of the non-organized community and the State, stress its survival and illustrate how diversification activities, subsequent to the listing stage, bring benefits to the enterprise in the form of greater stability of the resulting flow, reducing risks for investors. Thus, diversification reduces specific risk and contributes to reducing the expected yields by the financing entities in the absence of rationality hypotheses and perfect diversification of the asset portfolio.

Regarding the nature of sources and their relationship, it can be stated that after the first capitalization stage due to the issue of stock, the listed enterprise will be able to and must increase its use of financial leverage. This will take place by using new and more "powerful" debt instruments available to the listed companies. These securities issues, which are very different from one another, contribute to increasing the D/E ratio, which will return again to the alert level. In the final stages of this period, it will be possible to resort to operations with greater financial risk by issuing high risk non-guaranteed bond-backed loans, such as high yield bonds.

Continuing on its growth path, the enterprise enters into the **maturity stage**. This stage is characterized mainly by risks of a non-operating nature. The objectives at this stage are: stabilization of income flows, reduction of the cost of money, identification of rejuvenation operations (Baden, Fuller and Stopford, 1994) of activities associated with new products or markets, or even just new manufacturing processes.

As the enterprise matures, the expected yield of projects to be consummated will decrease following lack of more remunerative projects, with the consequent lower differential profitability of marginal projects compared to those initially undertaken. This circumstance, efficiently measured by a reduction of project Economic Value Added (Stewart, 1991), has the consequence of training management (Jensen, 1986) in the use of financial sources (Myers, 1984) especially in directing it toward operations that reduce the cost of money. This promotes the replacement of equity with third-party capital and indirectly increases the enterprise's insolvency risk. Management will also carry out risk hedging operations, transferring to third parties the so-called insurable risks and keeping only those typical and unavoidable enterprise risks. It emerges that the static vision of the enterprise does not contribute to the knowledge of the organic relationship existing among investments, financing, risk and yields required by the lenders. The enterprise, in its evolution, is transformed into investments and sources that ensure its coverage. At different stages of investments, operating risks with regard to projects carried out, logistics, manufacturing and marketing of goods and services emerge.

Financial risk originates from the sources and it is characterized from insolvency risk, but other financial risks linked to the characteristics of raised financing are associated with it such as interest rate and foreign exchange risks.

Table 1.2: Enterprise Development Cycle, Types of Business Risks, and Performance of the D/E Debt Ratio.

	Start-up	Expansion	Going Public	Public	Maturity
Development Stage	Start-up	Expansion	Going Public	Public	Maturity
Nature of Investments	Investments in organization of manufacturing and adaptation functions	Commercial expansion, plant and machinery	M&A	—	—
Nature of Sources	Initial equity contribution + bank debt	Prevailing bank debt on net assets. Pre-IPO potential and mezzanine	Net assets raised in IPO, senior structured debt	Net assets (increases), Senior debt, secondary and subordinated.	Low yield debt
Enterprise Risks	Enterprise organizational operating risks	Operating and financial risk	Operating, financial and regulatory risk	Prevailing financial risk	Financial risk and governance risk
D/E Ratio	Low-increasing / High	Low-recapitalization / High	Low / High	Very high	Very high
D/E					

Risk and Enterprise Value

Business studies and in particular Corporate Finance have attempted to link enterprise risks to the yields required by its lenders. The theoretical models and operating tools were introduced to understand, assess and then reduce enterprise risks (Doherty, 1985; Greene and Serbein, 1983; Ferry, 1988). As we will see in greater detail in Chapter 2, these pigeonholing efforts lead to the inception of a line of studies known as **corporate risk management** in which the relationship between risk and enterprise value is assumed as primary, and activities are organized to place the traditional objective of maximization of enterprise value next to the peculiar, that are sought after for the objective of risk minimization.

For decades, Corporate Finance has assumed the task of investigating the relationship between risk and value. This has led to studies on the adequacy of the economic and financial structure of the enterprise when performing its activities. Thus, from a financial perspective, the enterprise can be seen as the sum of its investments in assets and corresponding to the necessary financing for their coverage. In its operation, it is a body able to produce positive financial flows that exceed negative ones.

This description of the enterprise from its financial perspective indicates a close relationship between the enterprise's assets/investments and the financial sources which allows them to be carried out and take risk. Below are references to the origin of the relationship described above.

In 1927 at Ca' Foscari, Gino Zappa introduced business studies to the concept of enterprise income and built an enterprise theology for its maximization. In the same period, on the other side of the Atlantic, income was the subject of studies by equally illustrious economists and mathematicians. It was in 1930 that Irving Fisher announced the theory of interest and made a fundamental theoretical contribution to the development of management studies and, involuntarily, to Zappa's enterprise theology by introducing the concept of savings and investment and defining capital value and enterprise value and of other investments in relation to the income.

Although his interest was mainly focused on understanding the reasons for the existence of an interest rate on capital, indirectly, he shed light on the relationship between present savings, its "useful allocation" (investment) and yield or future income which could be drawn from invested savings. Fisher stated: *"Savings brings us to the nature of capital"*. It is in fact capital together with the interest rate applied to it that is linking element between present savings and future income. In the words of the American economist: *"Capital, in the sense of capital value, is simply discounted future income or, in other words, capitalized"*. Thus, Fisher clearly links the concept of present savings with that of future capital value, stating that: *"the value of any property, or rights to wealth, is its value as a source of income and it is found by discounting that expected income"* (Fisher, 1930, p. 26).

Thus, the foundations were laid for the value theory later developed by Modigliani and Miller (1958, 1963), Miller (1977) and by all scholars who contributed in making it in our time, the prevailing paradigm in management sciences (Rappaport, 1986; Stewart, 1991).

In 1930, Fisher was aware of the relationship existing between the current value of capital and uncertain future income.

"The basic problem of time valuation which Nature sets us is always that of translating the future into the present, that is, the problem of ascertaining the capital value of future income. The value of capital must be computed from the value of its estimated future net income, not vice versa" (Fisher, 1930, p. 31).

With these statements he showed his awareness that investment decisions are subject to the result of risk and uncertainty, leading to the conclusion that the enterprise value also depended on uncertainty and risk. This is certainly another fundamental factor whereby Fisher's contribution remains at the basis of the development of Corporate Finance: the introduction of "uncertainty and therefore of risk in determining enterprise value".

Subsequent scholars continued the work starting from this contribution and already with Modigliani and Miller (1958) and later with Myers (1984) and others the origin of value was further analyzed. In the eighties (Rappaport, 1986) the value paradigm became predominant. The enterprise's objective is that of maximizing value for shareholders. This objective is feasible and desirable when operating in conditions of certainty and uncertainty. We want to demonstrate in this paragraph how maximizing value can be attained at conditions of uncertainty and therefore how risk influences the objective function (Damodaran, 2006) of Corporate Finance.

Beginning from the concept of the enterprise specifically on the concept of investment introduced by Fisher (1930), an enterprise can be valued as the sum of the investment projects which an entrepreneurial economic entity carries out in order to accomplish its own "enterprise".

Substantially the value of any investment J, and therefore the sum of the enterprise, may be determined as value of future income flow (CF_t) generated by investment projects and implemented at an interest rate r which takes into account the degree of risk inherent in the evaluation

Formalizing:

$$W_{\mathrm{assets}} = \sum_{j=0}^{j} W_{\mathrm{project}_j} = \sum_{t=0}^{T} \frac{CF_t}{(1+r)^t}. \tag{9}$$

The components for determining value therefore are mainly three: cash flow generated by investment CF_t, time t and the discount rate r.

Under conditions of certainty, these variables have a univocal determination as they are certain values. This makes it possible for the enterprise value to be defined as the sum of nominal cash flows discounted at the risk free rate. Hence, instead of operating under conditions of uncertainty, things change. Univocally determined values will be replaced by estimates of variables and to do so, the respective frequency distributions of risk variables must be constructed for each element of the calculation.

In scholarship (Damodaran, 2011), the risk is included in the value formula by two alternative methods. The first requires the risk to be included in the estimated discount rate and for cash flows, instead of indicated at their nominal value. The second method requires the risk to be forecast and included in the estimate by weighing nominal flows with their probability of occurring. In this case, the literature deals with certain equivalent cash flow. Next to these two methods, there is also the "Venture Capitalist Method" (Callow, 2005), whereby the risk-adjusted expected yield is further divided by the probability of its occurrence.

Recently, the borrowing of risks management tools for the banking enterprises is an attempt to introduce the valuation of unexpected risk on non-banking operations using *Cash Flow at Risk*.

Inclusion of Risk in the Discount Rate

As mentioned above, in the first method of inclusion of uncertainty in discount rates, income flows (cash flows) are expressed in nominal terms which does not take into account the possibility that actual each flow may change due to the risk of the project. Risk, a consequence of uncertainty in which the decision is made, is included in the denominator of the formula described above, in which the interest rate at which cash flows are discounted and capitalized contains a premium for the risk. This rate will

Table 1.3: Method for Including Risk in the Enterprise Value Formula.

Criteria/CF and Rates Used	Certain Equivalents	Expected at Risk Flows	Venture Capital Method
Type of Flow to be Discounted	Certain equivalent of expected income	Average expected income	Outcome of the successful scenario
Discount Rate	Risk free	RAdR	Required yield
Calculated this Way	r_f	$r_f + $ risk premium	RAdR/probability of success of scenario

Source: Our formulation from Guatri and Bini (1998, p. 297).

always be estimated by taking into account the yield required by investors for giving up the use of their money and investing in an asset at risk. For this reason a performance premium must be added to the above-mentioned risk-free rate to indemnify the investor for the risk incurred in carrying out the project. This rate, known in the literature as *Risk Adjusted Rate of Return*, RAdR (Damodaran, 2011; Guatri and Bini, 1998), must take into account both operating risks inherent in the initiative and the financial risk emerging from the financial structure selected by the enterprise and from other financial risks.

Substantially RAdR $= E(R_j) = r_f$ RAdR $= E(R_j) = r_f + \Delta r$, where Δr is the premium for operating under conditions of uncertainty in investment j.

The calculation of the discount rate takes place by obtaining the weighted average of the cost of financial sources that participate in covering the investment; the major ones are equity and third-party capital.

The literature on the subject of **cost of money** is ample and varied. Sharpe (1964), Lintner (1965), Miles and Ezzel (1980) developed the contributions already known under the name of "WACC Textbook" (the so-called weighted average cost of money) which has contributed to complete the theoretical picture already outlined by Modigliani and Miller (1958, 1963).

In general, cost of money is understood as the weighted average compensation paid to lenders. This value may be estimated in two different ways. The charge to each source through the rate-cost is calculated according to logic of cost borne; weighed with the relative weight of the source in the financial structure.

$$\text{WACC} = R_e \frac{E}{E+D} + R_d \frac{D}{E+D}, \tag{10}$$

where the two cost components are calculated according to the following logic:

R_e is generally estimated using the onerousness of equity sources [historical return on equity (ROE)];
R_d is calculated as the ratio between financial burdens borne and contracted financial debt.

Alternatively, the estimate can be carried out through rate-opportunity, most often used in the case of a perspective measurement, in which case alternative investments which the lenders had to forego in order to invest in the enterprise are considered as the basis of the calculation. Consequently, the formula is illustrated as follows:

$$\text{WACC} = K_e \frac{E}{E+D} + K_d \frac{D}{E+D}, \tag{11}$$

where the two cost components are calculated accordingly:

K_e is generally estimated using the CAPM method calculated with a *leveraged beta* taking into account the specific financial structure and the financial risk associated to it;
k_d is calculated as the sum of the risk free rate and a premium for financing associated to the rating and the financed entity's likelihood of default.

The sum $D + E = V$ represents the enterprise value and is equivalent to the total of the sources necessary to cover the financial requirement. The manager will identify the optimal mix of financing that allows for maximizing the enterprise value according to the *Discounted Cash Flow* (DCF) formula is illustrated as follows:

$$W_{\text{assets}} = \sum_{t=0}^{T} \frac{\text{FCFF}_t}{(1 + \text{WACC})^t}. \tag{12}$$

This objective, assumes the FCFF to be constant based on the considerations previously stated coinciding with the search for minimizing the above-mentioned cost of business capital (WACC).

Inclusion of Risk in Cash Flows

A second method for evaluating the risk of an enterprise is by using the *Certainty Cash Equivalent* method in which the risk associated with carrying out the project is included in the estimated cash flows. This approach uses the quantification of certain cash flow that an entity is willing to receive in exchange of an at-risk one. This amount is called CEQ and is placed in the numerator position of the sum of FCFF and discounted at the risk-free rate.

$$W_{\text{assets}} = \sum_{t=0}^{T} \frac{\text{CEQ}_t}{(1+r_f)^t}. \tag{13}$$

An indirect approach similar to the one described above is presented by Guatri and Bini (1998), which is calculated indirectly by reducing the value of at risk cash flows of the cost of coverage. By doing this it will be possible to discount the difference at the risk free rate. The limitation of this additional approach is that it can be applied only when coverage is perfect. Thus, an expression of value of this type is illustrated in the following manner:

$$\sum_{t=0}^{T} \frac{(\text{Risky cash flows}_t - \text{coverage cost}_t)}{(1+R_f)}. \tag{14}$$

Similar to the previous case, the discount rate to be used in the valuation process of future flows is that of the risk-free investment. In fact, no premium for risk will be owed because the risk has already been calculated and participated in determining the numerator.

Inclusion of Risk in Cash Flows at Risk (CFaR)

Recently scholars have developed certain forecasting methods for at-risk cash flows. Among the better known, even though infrequently used in practice, is the Monte Carlo method. Next to it, an estimate method has been developed which we can describe as a derivative. In fact it originates from the estimate of the *Value at Risk* (VaR). VaR may be used in the analysis of enterprise risk and it allows us to give a value to the latter based on CFaR. This method attempts to include in the calculation those variables that allow the measuring of the volatility of operating cash flows of a commercial nature rather than concentrating on the variability introduced by market risks as in VaR. In the literature, three separate methods are known for calculating CFaR. The first is the traditional method developed by Risk Metric (1999) and it is known as the *Bottom–up* method; there is also a method illustrated by Stein, Ulsher and Laguttata (2001) defined as the

Top–down. Recently, a third method has been developed called *"Exposure Base CFaR"* (Andrén, Jankensgard and Oxelheim, 2005).

The *Bottom–up* method performs an estimate of CFaR in which it tries to identify and measure the volatility components exposed to market risks. The definition of CFaR focuses on knowing the volatility of cash flows at a given level of the market risk. This approach can be used when the top management is reasonably sure of its assessments regarding risk and is especially aware of the mechanisms when the market risk will change leading to a modification of cash flows. This is the principal limitation, which allowed the development of alternative approaches. The *Top–down* method builds the distribution of probability from historical business data and subjective projections and estimates of the managers from a large number of corporations. This approach has the advantage of offering a historical average estimate of risk exposure. This estimate must reflect the experience of a plurality of enterprises exposed to market risk in ways that can even be dissimilar.

The strong point of this method is its main limitation. In fact, the enterprises used for constructing the distribution of probability can be very different from one another and therefore, lead to results unusable by the enterprise with CFaR to be examined. The authors (Stein, Ulsher, and Laguttata, 2001) observing approximately 85,000 enterprises included in the Compustat database, and in particular trying to explain unexpected variations of the EBITDA of these enterprises, reach the conclusion that the said variations can mainly be attributed to four different groups of variables: size, profitability, an indicator of sector risk for cash flows and finally the volatility of the stock price. Based on these categories, they divided enterprises into homogeneous groups and constructed the distributions of probability of cash flows by homogeneous categories.

To remedy the low level of attention given to both the previous methods, which are based on an estimate of CF variability of the market variables, the *Exposed Based-CFaR* method offers a third calculation method consisting of six stages:

(1) Identification of expected macroeconomic and market variables relevant for the purpose of performance;
(2) Acquisition and generation of forecasts of macroeconomic and market variables relevant for an estimate of volatility;
(3) Estimate of the *"Exposure Model"* as plausible from an economic standpoint as its statistical characteristics are valid;

(4) Simulation of values pertaining to macroeconomic variables using random values extracted from the variance–covariance matrix;

(5) Inclusion of the above values in the model to generate conditional distribution of the cash flow taking into account the impact of macroeconomic market variables alone and the frequency distribution constructed considering all the unidentifiable variables as sources of non-macroeconomic volatility;

(6) Combination of the two frequency distributions into a single distribution to identify the degree of confidence with which to calculate CFaR.

The last method was developed almost exclusively in medium–large industrial enterprises in which it clearly identifies which part of the cash flow variability is attributable to macroeconomic and market risks and which one is not attributable to them.

Thus, this method approaches risk handling in accordance with the principles of the financial portfolio theory (Markowitz, 1952; Modigliani and Miller, 1958; Sharpe, 1964) and gives an independent dimension to systematic and specific risk borne by the enterprise.

Chapter 2

RISK MANAGEMENT: ANALYSIS OF RISK, ENDOWMENT CAPITAL, AND SUPPLIERS OF FINANCE

Oliviero Roggi

Evolution of Risk Management (RM) Studies and Treatment of Pure Risks

For many decades, RM has been at the center of a growing number of studies and analyses aimed at understanding and reducing the effects of risk on the enterprise. The objective of these studies and the tools that have evolved over time has encompassed increasingly new groups of risks. As a result, RM has become an interdisciplinary perspective with experts from the fields of banking, corporate financing, enterprise statisticians and actuarial mathematicians. It has become a branch of social sciences that studies the occurrence of risks, whether pure and/or speculative. However, these two types of risks have encountered different levels of attention from various scholars.

Initially, scholars analyzed the nature and occurrence of pure risks and, with the help of tools from actuarial science, they helped in setting the hedging strategies. The works of Dennenberg and Ferrari (1966), Blinn and Brown (1982), Willet (1951), Williams and Heins (1964) fall into this line of studies. They systematized the nature and probability of the occurrence of negative events for the enterprise and established the processes for analysis and hedging of pure risks.

When the economic sciences started to specialize in better defined disciplines, the managerial sciences developed RM which has a comprehensive and integrated framework for managing risk in the organization. This new field of study started to be called **Corporate Risk Management** (**CRM**) *or Enterprise Risk Management* (**ERM**).[1] Before the emergence of such studies, general and micro economists (Fisher, 1930; Markowitz, 1952; Modigliani and Miller, 1958, 1963; Fama, 1970; Fama and French, 1984; Jensen, 1986; Miller, 1977; Myers, 1984) have developed their theoretical models and operating tools to understand, assess and reduce enterprise risks (Floreani, 2005; Dickinson, 2001, p. 360). In the mid-1990s, these systemizing efforts gave birth to enterprise risk planning, a practice that was neglected before. The relationship between risk and enterprise value are assumed in which the principal and the managers incorporate the traditional objective of maximization of enterprise value with risk minimization. According to Nocco and Stulz (2006), ERM recognizes the imperfection of markets, diversification of investment portfolio and other imperfections that step away from the world designed by the neoclassical finance, and allows the enterprise to create value by reducing risks.

ERM analyzes risks arising from the economic–financial enterprise decisions. These decisions are made under conditions of uncertainty. The entrepreneur is required to make investment decisions, to bear risks, given the asynchrony existing between negative cash flows generated by the acquisition of manufacturing factors (*Capex and working capital*) and positive cash flows associated with selling products on the market to non-organized individuals. These decisions are subject to the ERM that aims to manage and reduce enterprise risk respecting the shareholder value theory's objective of maximizing the enterprise value. Hence, it is possible to measure the impact of enterprise value generated by the active management of business risks and the increases in value following risk assessment processes. This value is defined as "hedging benefit" and it assumes a value equal to zero when the market is perfect and risk is passed from the enterprise to its lenders without being modified.

RM and Typical Intervention Areas

CRM, also well known as ERM, can be defined as a strategic support activity to the enterprise management, which aims to create business value

---

[1]In the remainder of the discussion (report) they used the two definitions as synonyms.

in favor of the shareholders through an integrated process of identification, estimation, assessment, handling and control of all business risks. The CRM is an organizational process developed according to the guiding principle of neoclassical finance of value maximization. Specifically, the subject of that process is the enterprise risk as mentioned in the section *"Retained Risk and the Role of Equity as Guarantee Fund for Fighting Against Uncertainty"* (p. 59) which materializes as business and/or leverage risk.

Traditional Risk Management (TRM)

TRM (Olson and Wu, 2008) is known in the literature as the first type of techniques used in the field of risk forecasting and hedging. Its general objective is handling pure risks that may arise during the life of an enterprise. TRM is considered a subset of ERM because it identifies, measures and handles downside risk only. For this reason, most of contributions are on pure risk coverage tools and techniques. In fact, risk prevention, protection and coverage assume relevance through the transfer to third parties (insurance policies and other risk transferring tools). This TRM approach contributes to value creation and to value maximization by minimizing downside risk. In this direction the contributions are known as *"crisis management"* (Coombs, 1999; Seeger and Sellnow, 2007) and *business continuity management.* Compared to *ERM*, the approach has a narrow scope and identifies a limited number of risk sources and it is affected by a lack of coordination with other type of risks (e.g., speculative risk, strategic risk).

Project Risk Management (PRM)

PRM is the process whereby risks associated with large public or private structures are identified, analyzed and handled (Pennock and Haimes, 2002; Williams 1995; Bing and Tiong, 1999). Given the aforementioned characteristics, this stream of studies has a limited range of action than ERM and is employed in the construction industry of large public works or in the advanced mechanical industry (Aeronautics, Space, and also Naval). Here the objective is to build and manage processes in order to limit the downside risks generated during the execution of the project. When dealing with major structures which are complex in their execution, risk sources are mainly business ones: i.e., the risk of service interruption due to meteorological events, geological risks, and all operating risks. The occurrence of the above-mentioned risks and those typical for a complex project has the effect of modifying the estimates of expected positive cash flows.

The project may also incur financial risks, due to the effect of certain market risks. In particular, risk of liquidity deriving from a delay in the progress report payments; or that of interest rate or foreign exchange rate in the case of foreign currency flows.

Financial Risk Management (FRM)

FRM (Chapman, 2011) analyzes the enterprise financial risks. This approach to RM has received approval among industrial enterprises following the introduction of derivative products mainly on foreign exchange and interest rates. Conti (2006) demonstrates this by adapting the concept to non-financial enterprises. He refers to corporate FRM as: "the study which has as its subject the management of price-related financial risks (interest rate, foreign exchange rate, price of commodities, etc...) in non-financial enterprises" (Conti, 2006, p. 1). Because of the large variety of new tools introduced on the derivative market, FRM uses powerful financial products for mitigating risks originating from market variables linked to choices of investment and financial structure. Similar to TRM, it focuses only on some enterprise risks and it appears as a subset of the techniques provided in ERM.

The RM Process

In the Association of Insurance and Risk Managers in Industry and Commerce (AIRMIC)[2] definition (2002, p. 2), **RM** is defined as "the process through which institutions handle risks associated with the activities carried out, with the objective of obtaining benefits pertaining to the individual activities and/or the activities as a whole".

The process certified by AIRMIC requires the analysis to be carried out in four sequential stages (Figure 2.1):

(1) *Definitions of RM and enterprise objectives*;
(2) *Risk assessment*;
(3) *Risk treatment*;
(4) *Risk monitoring*.

Some of the previous stages are broken down into sub-stages. Out of the main stages, some have prevalently regulatory managerial contents,

---

[2]Association of Insurance and Risk Managers. http://www.airmic.com.

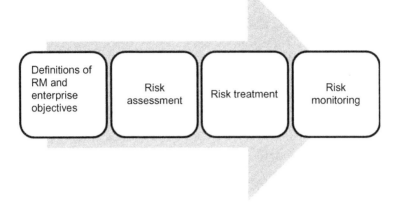

Figure 2.1: The RM Process.
Source: Our formulation.

whereas other stages are mainly technical. Among the managerial stages, "the selection of RM objectives", which are strategic enterprise objectives and the risk treatment stage, presupposes a definition of decisional criteria for handling risk and therefore is shaped as a typical activity in enterprise government. The other stages of the process are technical and include risk assessment, risk reporting and monitoring.

In general, the RM process (Shimpi, 2001, p. 59) helps the enterprise to:

(1) Define risks bearable by the enterprise;
(2) Develop a catalog of potential risks, which allows the enterprise to include a dynamic financial model with the effects of the principal risks identified, transferred or held.

Identification of the Enterprise's Goals in Term of RM

This phase is performed by the top management and begins with the identification of an *ex-ante* firm's policy about the various forms of potential risks. In addition to setting the objectives in terms of sustainable risk, financial planning is done for financing the RM process. For this reason, management is called on to define strategic objectives, first, operational goals and, finally, to organize their action plans about risk consistent with the shareholder maximization approach.

The risk strategy set during this phase should be compatible with the degree of risk a version of the shareholders. Keynes (1930) considers this as an intrinsic and a genetic characteristic of the decision-making of individuals and enterprises.[3]

In this context, every RM decision must be analyzed by answering the following question: "What impact does the hedging or retention action have on the value of the enterprise for its shareholders?" Only in this way RM and CRM can be used as strategic leverage in the creation of enterprise value.

Risk Assessment

The second phase is divided into three sub-phases:

(a) Risk identification/description
(b) Risk estimation
(c) Risk assessment

Risk identification/description

In the identification phase, the enterprise risks are listed and described by looking at the sources of potential negative outcome capable of compromising the achievement of the company objectives. Losses can impact enterprise's plans as a whole, or only certain activities it undertakes. Hence, to know the variability on the economic-financial results and its solvency, analysts need to break down the business of the enterprise or its plans into elementary units within which risks can be easily identified. To help in the identification process, the sources are classified into external/internal and risks into pure risks and speculative risks. Clearly, the emphasis is placed on identifying downside risk and only after that the analyst can spend time in listing the upside risk capable of bringing beneficial effects on economic-financial performance and/or the capitalization of the enterprise.

The RM analyst identifies risks using various collection methods. Primarily he/she uses the past history of losses taking all information

---

[3]Keynes (1930) claims in his famous book "*The General Theory of Employment, Interest and Money*":

> "*Even apart from the instability due to speculation, there is the instability due to the characteristic of human nature that a large proportion of our positive activities depend on spontaneous optimism rather than mathematical expectations, whether moral or hedonistic or economic. Most, probably, of our decisions to do something positive, the full consequences of which will be drawn out over many days to come, can only be taken as the result of animal spirits — a spontaneous urge to action rather than inaction, and not as the outcome of a weighted average of quantitative benefits multiplied by quantitative probabilities*" (pp. 161–162).

on negative events occurring in the enterprise. Similar to every historic analysis, it is not possible to identify new risks nor those present in the past that did not manifest themselves. The operator can use interview and brainstorming with key persons of the production and entry process of the business to obtain, through a structured questionnaire, a concrete map of possible negative events. Normally, the operators use actual prompt lists in which risks are classified according to uniform categories. The contents of these lists are generally developed during the analysis of similar enterprises that were previously subjected to an investigation by the operator.

To complete the mapping of risks once the events' losses are identified, it is necessary to describe the risks that the enterprise is subjected to. In this second task of the identification phase, the risk checklist contains the following information: type of risks, qualitative description of risk, principal up/downside scenarios linked to the probability of occurrence, and a summary evaluation of the economic consequences for each scenario. The checklist indicates the subjects responsible for managing each risk.

Risk estimation

Once the map (checklist) is known, the enterprise must work on a set of measures capable of quantifying the probability of the event and its impact on cash flows, estimating unexpected losses and/or the excess returns. Estimation methods are divided into three main groups based on the nature of the estimate:

(a) Qualitative estimates;
(b) Semi-quantitative estimates;
(c) Purely quantitative estimates.

Qualitative estimates differ from others as the result is not given in terms of the probability of an event. It is expressed by a qualitative scale that illustrates the intensity of the relationship. The second semi-quantitative estimate is preferable to the first and to the other quantitative estimates when a synthetic numerical indicator (scoring) is needed, but it is not necessary to quantify the probability distribution of a loss. Quantitative estimates such as the Monte Carlo simulation, determine an estimate for the probability distribution of a risk. Let's look at the differences in detail.

Purely qualitative risk estimation

Qualitative methods use descriptive words or scales to illustrate the economic effects and the realization probabilities of a risk event.

The **Probability–Impact matrix**, also known under the name of "P–I matrix" is the most popular method used to determine the qualitative estimates of pure risks defined by:

— A qualitative scale that indicates the probability of the occurrence of a given risk event. Generally, there are five impact classes (insignificant–low–moderate high–catastrophic);
— A qualitative scale representing the impact, or the possible economic consequences arising from the risk event. There are generally five probability classes (almost certain–probable–moderate–improbable–rare);
— A qualitative scale assigns every combination of elements (probability–impact) a rating risk. This can have four different values (extreme–high–moderate–low);
— An appropriate criteria for risk rating assessment.

The matrix can be represented by Table 2.1.

It is worth emphasizing that the scales and risk rating criteria depend on discretionary choices of the Corporate Risk Officer (CRO). To achieve a qualitative estimate, the risk manager might use brainstorming sessions, conduct interviews, or decide to have the P–I matrix prepared directly by the officer-in-charge of the particular risk.

Table 2.1:   The Structure of the P–I Matrix.

Probability	Impact				
	Insignificant	*Low*	*Moderate*	*High*	*Catastrophic*
Almost Certain (>50%)	High	High	Extreme	Extreme	Extreme
Probable (20–50%)	Moderate	High	High	Extreme	Extreme
Moderate (5–20%)	Low	Moderate	High	Extreme	Extreme
Improbable (1–5%)	Low	Low	Moderate	High	Extreme
Rare (<1%)	Low	Low	Moderate	High	High

Note: Low: The risk is managed using routine procedures; Moderate: Requires the identification of the person in charge for managing and monitoring the risks following in this class; High: Careful risk evaluation by the Chief Risk Officer; Extreme: Requires a maximum level of attention, and an immediate intervention for risk treatment.

Once the general pattern is defined, the classification of risks in the P–I matrix is performed. This is a key operation performed by the CRO. As a result, special care should be used in classifying a risk. As it relates to the principal pros and cons of the P–I matrix, it is possible to claim that it is very simple to be prepared and used, while on the other hand, it can be considered an initial screening of pure risks and cannot be used in the case of speculative risks. A limit to the use of qualitative estimates is that it is used to attribute a single evaluation to random variables that have the same anticipated value, but differentiated risks. That depends on the P–I method, which tends to combine a quantitative variable such as probability through a single parameter, though not objective parameter such as a rating risk.

Purely semi-quantitative risk estimation

A semi-quantitative estimate[4] is a method in which a series of qualitative judgments are transformed in quantitative variables through the use of scoring systems or functions and mathematic scaling methods to arrive at a synthetic risk judgment. In this method, the operator limits himself to order risks through assigning scores that measure the intensity of risk. This is possible by applying a score or a mathematical function to the qualitative scale. This method is known as the risk score, and is applied to the "P–I matrix" (see Table 2.2). All of the risk scoring methods, including the famous Altman model (1968), are based on this method and can be effectively used in the evaluation of risks while taking into account a number of objective variables and comparative evaluations of multiple random sources (Crouhy, Galai and Mark, 2000). Semi-quantitative methods attempt to mitigate one of the principal limits of the qualitative method, that is, the impossibility to perform an economic convenience analysis.

Among the limits assigned to this family of methods, the main factor is not to permit the choice between investments based only on the score (X) obtained. Another additional limit is not being adequate in the evaluation of upside risks and not being able to fully estimate pure risks. The very last negative factor is represented by the limiting risk analysis to a single severity index. This entails a significant loss of information, as all available information must be summarized as a single number.

---

[4]For an in-depth analysis of semi-quantitative estimated methods: See Crouhy, Galai, and Mark (2000); Vose (2000); Corvino (1996); Cameron and Raman (2005).

Table **2.2**:   Example of the Risk Score Method.

Probability	Score
Almost certain	100
Probable	50
Moderate	25
Improbable	5
Rare	1

Impact	Score
Catastrophic	1000
High	200
Moderate	50
Low	10
Insignificant	1

Risk Score	
Extreme	$X > 5000$
High	$500 < X < 5000$
Moderate	$50 < X < 500$
Low	$X < 50$

Source: Our formulation.

The Risk Score method, which is applied to the P–I matrix, represents only one of the methods. A possible variant could be applied to the qualitative scale, as an ideal point of departure a mathematical function, as a domain of the categories of the scale.[5] That means that the expert must above all define the scale on which the evaluation will be performed, and then evaluate the frequency of each of them. This can be done by constructing a table like Table 2.3.

Table **2.3**:   Judgment Scale.

Judgment	Score
Unlikely	1.0–1.5
Improbable	1.5–2.5
Possible	2.5–3.5
Probable	3.5–4.5
Certain	4.5–5.0

Source: Carroll (1984).

The score value is then transformed into a probability value using the following function.

$$P(Z) = \left(\frac{\ln(Z)}{\ln(5)}\right)^4 . \tag{1}$$

---

[5]Carroll (1984).

Other semi-quantitative approaches also exist that tend to compress, if not eliminate entirely, the phase concerning the expression of a qualitative judgment in favor of a quantitative score. ***Fink Methodology*** provides a valid and correct demonstration of what has just been claimed.[6] The principal goal of this method is to estimate the circumstances in which relevant crisis events affect the firm's consolidated behavior and its relations with the stakeholders. The key questions under the Fink approach are:

— What is the maximum intensity that the crisis can reach?
— What is the average attention devoted to the crisis?
— To what extent can the crisis interfere with normal operations?
— To what extent can the crisis damage the corporate image?
— To what extent can the firm's financial resistance be put to the test?

Each question must be answered with a score between 0 and 10. The result of adding the values from each line is a number between 0 and 50, which expresses the seriousness level of the possible consequences of the crisis.

Regardless of the method used, we must emphasize how the semi-quantitative approach represents an improvement over simple qualitative estimates. Naturally, semi-quantitative evaluation is characterized by a number of rather significant limits worth remembering:

— It is a useful approach to evaluate pure risks, though it is not the case for speculative risks;
— It engages in excessive simplification using a single indicator for the seriousness of the event;
— The result is the output of an approximate analysis, which involves a significant loss of information.

In conclusion, it is useful to recall how in recent years an alternative/supplemental method has been identified for qualitative and semi-quantitative methods.

These methods can be used as an educational tool, especially when the audience comprises individuals without sufficient skills in the area of risk management to be able to fully understand the results of a quantitative analysis. Also, this kind of schematization makes it possible not to disseminate information to the general public.

---

[6]Fink (1984).

Pure quantitative risk estimates

The principal goal of quantitative methodologies[7] is to estimate the distribution of probability of random variables representing the company's risks.

There are two similar representations of the effect of risk on the enterprise:

— **The distribution of possible results**, which indicates the impact of a single risk on the firm's net profit/operating margin, assuming as axiom the neutrality of other business risks;
— **The distribution of possible losses**, which indicates the negative variation which a risk can cause on the maximization of profit. In this second distribution, the downside risk is given special attention.

As we have already indicated above, the quantitative estimate process consists in determining the possible results of an event. That is determined in a process in which the objectives of the review are set first, followed by a selection of the random variables. Finally, the statistical methodology is chosen that can perform the quantitative estimate of risk incurred by the enterprise. Table 2.4 contains a summary of the salient aspects of each phase.

The itinerary described in Table 2.4 represents a logical path to follow when the quantitative methodologies used are numerous and highly varied.

Alternatively, it is possible to use a well-known method in the analysis of investments, known as the **probability tree**. This method is based on the assumption that the potential frequency of the event being studied can be broken down into a series of sub-sequential events necessary for it to occur in which each is characterized by an autonomous probability of occurrence.

For the event to occur, it is necessary for a series of sub-events to take place. As a result, a relationship of the following type is created:

$$P(M) = P\left(\frac{M}{L}\right) \cdot P(M) + P\left(\frac{L}{I}\right) \cdot P(I) + P\left(\frac{I}{A}\right) \cdot P(I) + P(A),$$

or alternatively:

$$P(M) = P(M) \cap P(L) \cap P(I) \cap P(A).$$

---

[7]For an in-depth analysis on the subject of quantitative estimates, see the following sources: Cameron and Raman (2005); Crouhy, Galai, and Mark (2000); Vose (2000); Klugman, Panjer, and Willmot (1998); Allen (2003); Green and Serbein (1983).

Table 2.4: The Phases of the Quantitative Estimate Process.

Formulation of the Model	Represents a first step of fundamental importance. In this first phase it is necessary to reconcile the needs of simplicity and focus of the analysis, and those of *"realisticness"* and completeness. To accomplish this, the risk specialist can draw on a number of existing and proven models. The analysis is simplified by the monetary nature of the variables involved.
Determination of the Characteristics of the Random Variables and Principal Parameters of the Model	The determination of the characteristics of the random variables is identified by: — **Hypotheses or axioms on which to base the model**. In order to obtain a more rigorous analysis, it is necessary to use theoretical indications that provide an approximation of realty. — **Historical series and other information**. Through a careful analysis of the information provides a better knowledge and estimate than that of the relevant parameters of the model. — **Subjective evaluations done by experts**. This is an evaluation that can be used successfully in qualitative and semi-quantitative estimates during the identification phase of the principal risk factors. However, it is almost unusable in the case of quantitative estimates because there are problems in transforming a qualitative evaluation to a quantitative one.
Determination of the Distribution of the Possible Results and Summary Indicators	The determination of the model can be done by: — **Analytical resolution**. This represents the best solution when the distribution of the random variable under examination is identified directly by the model using the properties that characterize the random variable. However, the analytic solution represents a feasible path in the case of variables which are normally distributed. In fact, in all other cases, the use of other instruments is preferable. — **Monte Carlo simulation**. This is one of the most common methods for solving problems relating to the estimation of random variables. The Monte Carlo method consists of seeking the solution of a problem, by representing it as a parameter of a hypothetical population, and, in the estimate of this parameter by examining a sample taken from the population through a sequence of random numbers. In other words, it is possible to estimate the random variable objective by generating a sufficiently high number of random scenarios (or interactions) by which to create the frequency distribution.

(Continued)

Table 2.4:   (Continued)

	The Monte Carlo simulation provides for the realization of the following passages: — **Simulation of a random realization of the random variable objective**; — **N times repetition of the previous operation,** so as to arrive at N random realizations of the random variable objective; — **Estimate of the distribution of the random variable objective** through N random realizations; — **Estimate of the synthetic indicators of the variable.**
Validation and Verification of the Model	This is a phase aimed at verifying the validity of the results from the analysis performed.

The probability tree method allows us to break down a naturally complex problem into a series of elementary problems and it allows more detailed and better knowledge of the risk dynamics to determine an event characterized by highly negative impacts. It also makes possible to readily identify those measures suitable to avoid the occurrence of the loss.

Another well-known method is *Program Evaluation and Review Technique* (***PERT***).[8] The principle characteristic of this method is to provide a single indicator determined by the following equation:

$$Q = \frac{V_{Optimum} + 4\,V_{Probable} + V_{Pessimistic}}{6} \qquad (2)$$

where

— Q = quantity to estimate;
— $V_{Optimum}$ = value which the quantity can assume under the most optimistic estimate;
— $V_{Probable}$ = value which the random variable should assume with greatest probability;
— $V_{Pessimistic}$ = value which the quantity can assume under pessimistic estimate.

[8]See Fazar (1959); Malcolm, Roseboom, Clark, and Fazar (1959); Minty (1998); Stevenson (1996).

This method is based on a weighted average with $\{k = 1\}$ for the most extreme cases and $\{k = 4\}$ for the most probable case, which generally coincides with the intermediate value. It is possible to use different coefficients when using a series of estimates based on an historical analysis.

Enterprise Value and Risk Evaluation: The Economic Value Model

The identification of an economic-value model of risk allows us to specifically create a link between the value generated in RM and enterprise risk. In the first chapter, we illustrated how the link between risk and value has been vigorously debated in the literature. In this case, starting from the neoclassical finance model for which hedging transactions do not generate value, as a rational and highly diversified investor is subject only to systemic risks, we agree with those authors (Adam and Chitru, 2005; Stulz, 1996; Brown, Crabb and Haushalters, 2002; Henteschel, Kothari and Adam, 2005), who observe how market imperfections, and irrational behavior of operators, are potential elements generating value from the hedging. Essentially, ERM operates on the conviction that treating risks is a consistent top management activity compatible with the maximization of the corporate value and capable of generating additional wealth for shareholders. Coming to the illustration of the methods used to arrive at increased value through hedging, we observe how to arrive at an overall evaluation. The risk manager must use with discretion the results of the estimate of the individual risks identified above and insert them into a decision-making model. However, before treating the risks, their impacts must be measured in terms of the value created.

The Economic-Value Model

The decisions concerning risk treatment methods can only be taken through the preliminary construction of an **economic-value model** in which the probability distributions of the risk source variables are linked to the value of the enterprise.

The selection of the economic-value model must be performed by taking into account a set of dimensions that are not affected by the variability of the random variables used in estimating the corporate risks. The model must be **consistent with the strategic and management objectives of the enterprise** and must take into account the environment and the markets in which the enterprise or institution operates. Finally, it is necessary to understand the structure of the preferences of the enterprise's target markets.

Another limitation is the type of estimates used. If they are qualitative or semi-quantitative, it will not be possible to trace the decisions to retention/alienation/treatment to arrive at consequences in terms of incremental cash flows without recurring to the skills of the evaluator. However, estimates of a quantitative nature are used and the economic-value model will allow at understanding whether the risk treatment will or will not generate cash flows.

The literature contains many models capable of quantifying incremental flows. Financial management scholars interested in evaluating market imperfections use the following process:

(1) **Estimate the distribution of Incremental Risky Cash Flows (IRCF$_t$)**[9] linked to the risk that is being evaluated (for instance, the size of the premium paid to t_0 to hedge a certain risk) to which are being **added the cash flows derived from compensation** in case of loss. The probability of occurrence will be applied to each of the possible loss manifestations. It will be possible to arrive at E(IRCF$_t$);

(2) These risky cash **incremental flows** will be **discounted to the risk free rate**;

(3) The **systematic risk** of the investment will be taken into account adjusting these flows to the variability introduced by it.

The algebraic sum of the two addenda determined above, PV (IRCF$_t$) + Δ systematic risk gives the Fair Value.[10] If the market in which

---

[9]Incremental risky cash flows are characterized for being exclusively operational in nature, and they do not have to take into account the implications of the financial structure or financial charges and income depending in some way on the decision to hedge risk. IAF also do not include indirect costs linked to the occurrence of an unfavorable event such as the greater costs of raising the liquidity necessary to meet the negative event which however is already estimated in the negative incremental flows.

[10]Fair Value can be defined, for this evaluative context only, as the current value of expected incremental risky cash flows is determined with the market value (price) they assume if traded on a perfect financial market. This is a value concept used by the theorists of neoclassical finance. The literature knows at least two different methods to determine Fair Value. The first is known as the portfolio method of the *replicant* widely used in the pricing of derivatives. See the main works on the valuation of options and their most recent applications. Merton (1973), Black (1975), Black and Scholes (1973), Hull (2006), Roll (1977). However, the second is determined on the basis of incremental risky cash flows, flows include the correction necessary to consider the systematic risk incurred by a well-diversified investor. Another meaning of Fair Value is mainly use in

the risk appears were complete and perfect and investor behavior rational, Fair Value would measure the contribution of the hedging decision to the enterprise value. However, in cases where there are imperfections it will be necessary to algebraically add to the Fair Value, the incremental cash flows generated by the imperfections and the idiosyncratic (non-systematic) risks as well as the economic consequences of the imperfect diversification of the investment portfolio held by the shareholder. In this case, the process must continue;

(4) **Adjustment for negative incremental risks (downside risk) and for the effect of imperfections (IE_t)**

To consider the adjustments described above, the final value of the risk decision will be the algebraic sum of Fair Value with the flows derived from the adjustments and the effects of the inclusion of the risk premium in the discount rate of cash flows. These adjustments are the consequence of negative incremental risks and enterprise characteristics. The principal market imperfections able to generate value throughout the hedging decision are: transaction costs for hedging operations and the risk shifting effect. The latter can be defined as the occurrence of opportunistic behavior which management can engage in to the detriment of its lenders and in favor of the shareholders. The imperfections capable of generating positive value for hedging include direct and indirect bankruptcy costs. These include costs of the crises prior to composition proceedings and those costs incurred for bankruptcy and tax asymmetries (Miller, 1977; Miles and Ezzel, 1980).

The Effects of Imperfections

The effects of imperfections can be measured using a concept introduced in the first chapter, the maximum potential loss (MPL). This effect can be calculated as the product of the incremental downside risk (IR) and the premium for imperfections (IP).

---

corporation accounting as the basic criterion for the valuation of assets. This valuation criterion concerns the valuation of the corporation assets in going concern. International accounting practice and, in particular, international accounting principles (IAS), tend to abandon the "cost criterion" in favor of "Fair Value." In fact, IAS 32 and IAS 39 define, as has already been said, "The amount at which an asset can be exchanged or a liability extinguished between aware and available parties in a transaction between third parties". Essentially, this is valuation at the value which can be defined "market," translated from the EC directives into "Fair Value".

We arrive at the following equation:

$$EI_j = IR \times IP, \tag{3}$$

where EI_j is the value of imperfections represented by the symbol ΔVI.

From the long process illustrated to this point, the hedging decision value equals the algebraic sum of the components described above.

$$\text{Hedging decision value} = \sum_{t=0}^{T} \frac{E(\text{IRCF}_t)}{(1+r_f)^t} + \frac{\text{FRS}_t}{(1+r_j)^t} + \Delta VI. \tag{4}$$

where $E(\text{IRCF}_t)$ is the present value of positive incremental risky cash flows; r_f is the risk-free rate; r_j is given by the sum of the risk free with the market risk premium, when Beta $= 1$; FRS_t are the negative incremental cash flows corrected for systematic risk and ΔVI is the algebraic sum of the effects of the imperfections that are favorable/unfavorable to the hedging decision and are peculiar of the enterprise that assumes it and of the period in which it occurs. The first two addenda form what we call the Fair Value.

The phase concludes with a decision to hedge or not hedge the risk.

Strategies and Tools for Managing Uncertainty (Risk Treatment)

Each risk that is identified, estimated and evaluated is the subject of a treatment decision. There are three potential outcomes of the treatment decision (as per Figure 2.2):

(1) The project analyzed generates risk that exceeds the limit of risk aversion set by the Chief Risk Officer (CRO). This makes realization of the project unsuitable and consequently the risk is not assumed (risk avoided);

(2) The project under investigation is economically sound and generates risks that can be managed and minimized. The risk will be treated (risk treated);

(3) The project in question generates risks, which cannot be transferred or eliminated through RM and in this case the risk will be retained (risk retained).

Shimpi (2001) claims that the decision-making entity components for a risk can be classified using an intensity scale that varies from non-assumption of risk (0) to the retention of risk without hedging (1).

Modification of Shimpi claims (2001, 16ff.), can broaden the range of the decisions to the four options described below, introducing risk reduction action.

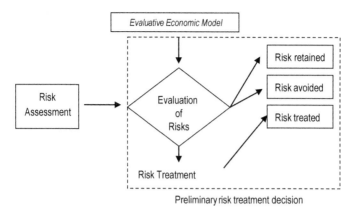

Figure 2.2: The Process for the Evaluation of a Risk Decision.
Source: Our adaptation from Shimpi (2001).

(1) *Risk avoidance*
(2) *Risk reduction*
(3) *Risk transfer*
(4) *Risk retention*

Therefore, it is preferable to reorganize the process according to the diagram (Figure 2.3):

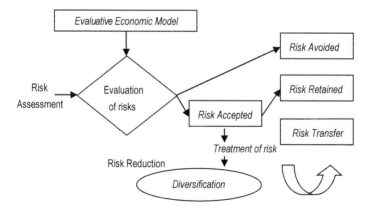

Figure 2.3: Risk Hedging Decisions.
Note: In italics risk-related decisions, in regular type the status of each analyzed enterprise risk.
Source: Our reformulation according to Shimpi (2001, p. 16).

The new aspect consists of the risk reduction phase, which is not contained in the previous model. This compels the broadening of the hedging process as follows: once identified and evaluated with an economic-financial model, the risks are alternatively avoided or accepted. In the case they are accepted they can be:

— Subject of retention. This way they are part of the portfolio risks incurred by the enterprise;
— Treated (risk treated) through risk diversification methods (risk reduction) or through transfer of risk to third parties (risk transfer).

Risk Avoidance

When the risks generated by a project are greater than those tolerable and are not consistent with the guiding objectives recommended in risk assumption, the manager will choose not to pursue the project, thus avoiding the resulting uncertainty (Risk Avoidance). In essence, these are projects for which the cost of hedging would be greater than the value generated by the project, which would entail a destruction of value. The threshold of acceptability depends on the risk propensity of the decision-making entity. If it were particularly low, it would result in the rejection of many projects presented. In this phase, the management's ability is to establish certain criteria for the determination of sustainable risk and holding it to maximize the value of the enterprise. Basically, the manager decider will exclude those risks that are difficult to evaluate or those that would compromise the results of the core business. Recalling the stream of literature base on risk-return, we can conclude that an enterprise that is strongly averse to risk, expects yields much lower than the one that accepts project risks. Risk avoidance is not suited to dynamic environments in which we have to continuously redefine markets, products, technology, which would lead to rejecting all projects.

Risk Transfer

In risk retention, a possible behavior in the case of the project able to create value and the risk worth taking is to transfer risk to a third party. The management may bound the risk retained by transferring it to other parties through the purchase of insurances or financial products and other atypical contracts that can reduce the variability of cash flows and limit the risk incurred. The risk transferred is typically the one in which hedging is convenient. A typical example of this behavior is the conduct adopted when faced with pure risks such as those of fire, insolvency of loans and every other event characterized by the presence of downside risk only. In the case of speculative risks, it will be necessary to create special hedging positions that can stabilize future cash flows (i.e., hedging again the fluctuation of the price of commodities such as oil, gas, gold, etc.). Recently, as Shimpi claims (2001, p. 19), hedging has extended to market financial risks such as exchange rate and interest rate risks.

Risk Retention

The last potential behavior toward risk indicated by Shimpi is the risk retention: the decision to assume the risk and to maintain it in the enterprise. This category of risks retained is made up of two distinct types of risk: the first, those that are assumed voluntarily by management; the latter, populated by all those risks the management was not able to identify, evaluate or decide whether or not to hedge. Shimpi states: "*A risk neglected is a risk retained*" (Shimpi, 2001, p. 19). It is precisely these unknown or unknowable risks that make it necessary to endow the enterprise with sufficient capital to meet the possible negative effects they generate.

Risk Reduction, Diversification, and Other Policies

The classification described above does not complete the list of actions available to the manager to reduce risk. In order to exhaust the list, it is necessary to cite risk reduction through an adequate portfolio diversification.

The objective is to reduce the retained risk as much as possible by using the reduction effect of the specific risk carried by undiversified investors. This method can be implemented either in *ex ante* (preventive) logic, or in an *ex-post* logic, to minimize the losses suffered when the event occurs.

The main tool used to reduce risk reduction is provided by the diversification policies introduced by Markowitz (1952) and developed by the scholars focused on risk-return ratio. Risk reduction is the phenomenon that occurs when a party owns a number of uncorrelated assets or negatively related ones, which results in a reduction of portfolio risk. In fact, the observed variance of the return of a diversified portfolio can be written as σ_p^2 and is determined as follows (Elton, Gruber, Brown, and Goetzmann,

2009, p. 53):

$$\sigma_p^2 = ER_p - (\tilde{R}_p). \tag{5}$$

When using only two securities, the deviations from the average value are:

$$ER_p - (\tilde{R}_p)^2 = E[W_1 R_1 - (\tilde{R}_1) + W_2 R_2 - (\tilde{R}_2)]^2. \tag{6}$$

It is necessary to take the square of the sum in the form

$$(a+b)^2 = a^2 + b^2 + 2ab.$$

Applied to the previous equation we obtain:

$$E\left[W_1 R_1 - (\tilde{R}_1) + W_2 R_2 - (\tilde{R}_2)\right]^2$$
$$= E\left[\begin{array}{c} W_1^2 R_1 - (\tilde{R}_1)^2 + W_2^2 R_2 - (\tilde{R}_2)^2 \\ + 2W_1 W_2 R_1 - (\tilde{R}_1)R_2 - (\tilde{R}_2) \end{array}\right]^2. \tag{7}$$

From which it follows that:

$$E\left[W_1^2 R_1 - (\tilde{R}_1)^2 + W_2^2 R_2 - (\tilde{R}_2)^2 + 2W_1 W_2 R_1 - (\tilde{R}_1)R_2 - (\tilde{R}_2)\right]$$
$$= W_1^2 E\left[R_1 - (\tilde{R}_1)^2\right] + W_2^2 E\left[R_2 - (\tilde{R}_2)^2\right]$$
$$+ 2W_1 W_2 E\left[R_1 - (\tilde{R}_1)R_2 - (\tilde{R}_2)\right], \tag{8}$$

or

$$\sigma_p^2 = W_1 \sigma_1^2 + W_2 \sigma_2^2 + 2W_1 W_2 \sigma_1 \sigma_2. \tag{9}$$

In this equation, the first two addenda estimate the variance of securities 1 and 2, each weighted with weights W_1 and W_2 squared; the third consists of twice the product of the weights for the covariance of security 1 with security 2. In conclusion, the variance of the portfolio consisting of two securities is determined on the basis of the variance of the securities taken individually, which is algebraically added twice the covariance.

The covariance takes on very high positive values whenever the securities are strongly related, and takes on a value of zero if the securities move independently. However, covariance takes on highly negative values if they move in the opposite direction.

The contribution provided by the covariances to the portfolio risk justifies the claim that by placing in portfolio assets that are independent or inversely related, it is possible to obtain a portfolio variance equal or lower than the sum of the securities variances. Hence, that determines the diversification effect.

It should be noted that diversification exhausts the risk reduction effect after the portfolio contains only 15–20 uncorrelated or inversely correlated assets. That is, the returns of the stocks listed on the same market are subject to sources of risk and the variability of common returns, such as: the cost of commodities, interest rates, inflation, and growth of the gross domestic product (GDP). This allows the recall of the distinction between diversifiable **risks** or risks **specific** to the investment and, on the other hand, non-diversifiable or **systemic** risks.

A rational, well diversified and marginal investor will be inclined to carry only systemic risks because specific risks can be reduced by resorting to a portfolio of uncorrelated assets. In doing so, diversification consists in a useful tool for risk reduction at least where the decision-maker has the possibility of splitting his portfolio in diversified assets.

Monitoring of Incurred Risks

The last phase of the integrated risk management process is monitoring. This phase requires both managerial and technical skills.

Scholars and experts on ERM agreed on the fact that monitoring is indispensable and that its subject is:

— **Monitoring of "retained" risks.** This is concomitant control on those business variables identified as potential sources of risk, risk which management has voluntarily decided to assume. Every deviation from the estimate of a risk must, in fact, contain a request by the decision maker who will undergo the monitoring;
— **Monitoring of the obsolescence of the results of the risk analysis.** This is because the environment is subject to change suddenly and unexpectedly;
— **Monitoring of the quality of the process and its effectiveness.** In this case the persons in charge of monitoring perform a test on the functioning of the risk management process by reporting and providing a solution for increasing efficiency to the top management.

Retained Risk and the Role of Equity as Guarantee Fund for Fighting Against Uncertainty

In the managerial literature retained risk is often identified with the **enterprise risk**. The presence of such risk is in fact inevitable and constitutes a founding element of each business that needs to anticipate investments in order to satisfy future of goods and services coming from the individuals. In this sense, it is understandable how the concept of risk is embedded in each enterprise. To cope with the risk and conduct business in an ongoing enterprise, the entrepreneur must obtain enough funding to finance the investments and to be able to repay the investors at maturity. Financial resources must be matched to the investments and the company should preserve in each moment of the life the financial equilibrium and the economic equilibrium at least in the long term.

In order to reach this status any corporation needs to raise enough equity to guarantee all third parties from future obligations. The equity should be sized depending on law prescription such as statutory equity, and voluntary raised equity (investment capital).

The enterprise cannot conduct its business solely with minimum statutory equity and due to the structure of its investments; it is characterized by much higher capital intensity. For this reason, it is necessary to raise new capital or retain dividend until an adequate level of capitalization is reached.

As described above, equity of a corporation consists of two addenda: statutory equity and voluntary capital.

Equity, Risk and Legal Guarantee

Since the pre-capitalist middle ages, the company equity has been identified as an amount anticipated by the entrepreneur for starting the production. David Ricardo,[11] states, "capital is the activating element of work capacity" (Ricardo, 1817).

Raised Capital is defined as the set of financial sources contributed by the shareholder enabling the enterprise to operate in conditions of financial equilibrium. Total equity includes raised capital (paid-in capital) and capital reserves accumulated over time, and other sources that can also be off-balance-sheet.

In this guarantee role, the capital raised or accumulated must be adequate to bear the negative effects of the occurrence of risks, which the enterprise generates while conducting of its business and also be able to guarantee financial equilibrium and to protect it from insolvency.

---

[11]For more detail see Ricardo (1817).

How much Capital the Firm Needs to Raise?

The size of paid-in capital and the relationship between this capital and debts are strategic decisions for those who wish to manage enterprise risk in an integrated way.

There are at least three needs for which the enterprise must have sufficient capital:

(1) Hedging operational investments → operational capital;
(2) Hedging expected and unexpected risks → venture capital;
(3) Market signals → signaling capital.

For each of these ends, it is necessary for the enterprise to endow itself with capital. The first, and most obvious, reason is to raise capital to fund the operational investments including both long-term and working capital. As we have seen in the previous chapter, a good second reason for having adequate capital is to protect against risks. In this sense, the enterprise must accumulate additional capital aimed at hedging the risks of expected and unexpected losses arising from the business activities. This second component is called venture capital. Finally, managers, in determining the optimal capital structure must also take in consideration the opinion of the financial market. This is why the so-called extra capital is collected with the sole intent of creating an available cash reserve to convince even the most skeptical of equity analysts, on the attractiveness of investing in the enterprise (signaling capital).

The Classical Model: All Risks are Transferred to the Suppliers of Finance

There is no clear consensus on the optimal amount of capital needed to guarantee financial equilibrium at all times. Practitioners and scholars studying indices and margin analysis have identified certain measures of solidity, stability and liquidity they assert as required to maintain the enterprise in equilibrium. Many accounting ratios provide guidance on appropriate capital, solvency and liquidity ratios to be maintained by firms. Financial analysts use industry "rules of thumb" to guide them in assessing the capital adequacy of firms. Some practitioners, analysts and researchers use complex models such as the financial center of gravity, precisely to study the dynamic relationship that exists between sources and uses of capital.

Capital Adequacy: Debt and Solvency Ratios
Cash flow/total debt
Interest coverage
Common equity as a % of total invested capital
Cash flow/current maturities of long-term debt
Total debt as a % of net working capital
Short-term debt as a % of total invested capital
Net worth as market value/total long-term liabilities
Current debt/net worth
Total equity/total assets
Total debt/total assets
Debt to equity ratio
Fixed assets to equity
Long-term debt as a % of total invested capital

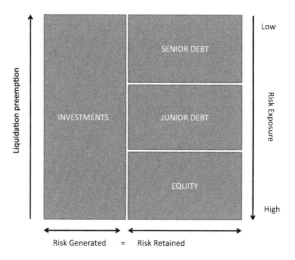

Figure 2.4:   The Standard Model for Determining the Financial Structure and the Relationship between Risk Generated and Risk Retained.

Source: Shimpi (2001).

However, all these approaches begin from a common initial considera-tion (see Figure 2.4). All of the risks generated by the enterprise activity are transferred to suppliers of finance (shareholders and bondholders). This means that the firm is risk neutral. In this scenario, the risk generated by the activities is equivalent to the risk retained by the supplier of finance. In fact, if the enterprise risk is not handled actively by management through risk management or diversification, then one can claim the equivalence between:

Risk generated = Risk retained.

The risk must fall on the supplier of total invested capital or paid-up capital: the sum of the financial sources actually paid-up within the enterprise.

Paid-up capital = F (Risk retained) = F (Risk generated).

In the classical approach, financial sources can be obtained in many ways. The three most common forms are equity capital, guaranteed debt or "senior debt" and subordinated debt. In addition to these forms we are increasingly finding mixed forms of semi-equity or quasi-equity which have specific debt characteristics and part equity characteristics. Equity, in turn, can be broken down into capital stock in the true sense and legal and voluntary reserves. These two aggregate into what is known as the enterprise's net assets.

Investments = Paid-up capital
= Senior debt + Junior debt + Equity.

The sources differ in terms of the risk exposure to the enterprise. Ordering the sources by increasing risk for the borrower (seniority), we find the senior loan, which is normally provided with real or personal collateral guarantees; then there is the junior loan, which is subordinated to the previous loan because the repayment rights are subordinated to those of the senior lenders. Finally, there is equity capital, for which shareholders expect repayment only in the case where repayment of capital and interest is made to the lenders. The shareholders are residual claimers and they bear, under ordinary conditions, the entire business and leverage risk.

This approach provides financing that carries the full risk generated by the enterprise. Generally, it is expected that equity holders bear all the expected losses of a firm. Therefore, the size of equity is a function of the maximum expected loss (at a particular level of confidence). On the basis of the above considerations, the enterprise risk falls simultaneously on all lenders (total invested capital or enterprise capital), while the effects of the loss are carried by shareholders' endowment capital. Lenders only suffer losses if the actual loss exceeds the expected loss and all the share capital is lost.

Then debt capital becomes impaired.

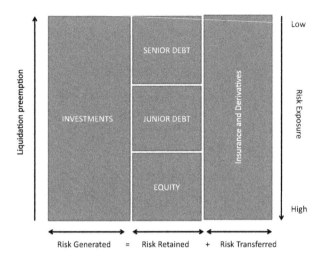

Figure 2.5:   The Insurance Model. Risk Total = Risk Retained + Risk Transferred.
Source: Shimpi (2001).

The Insurance Model

A more active approach to manage capital structure through active risk
management is known as *"the insurance model."* In the insurance model,
the risk generated by the enterprise (business and leverage risk) is in part
retained and in part transferred to third parties by entering into hedging
contracts (see Figure 2.5).

In this case, the risk generated by the investments (risk generated) is
offset by the risks retained and those transferred to third parties.

Risk generated = Risk retained + Risk transferred

The risk that falls on paid-up capital is in this case only a part of the
risk generated, leading to the need to collect a smaller capital share as a
consequence of the reduction of the MPL due to hedging. A second type
of capital can be transferred to third parties and constitutes off-balance-
sheet capital as a consequence of the transfer. Off-balance-sheet capital,
together with paid-up capital make up the guaranteed funds that cover
the risks generated by the enterprise (see also Figure 2.6).

$$\text{Paid-up capital} = F \text{ (Risk retained)}$$

$$\text{Off-balance-sheet capital} = F \text{ (Risk transferred)}$$

$$\text{Paid-up capital} + \text{Off-balance-sheet capital}$$

$$= F \text{ (Risk retained; Risk transferred)}$$

The *contingent capital*

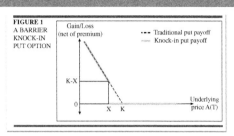

Definition: *"Contingent capital is a capital management tool that enables a company to draw upon a reserve pool of money, providing protection from the financial ramifications of an unforeseen event, such as a natural disaster or severe market correction"*

Culp 2002, Contigent Capital: Integrating corporate financing and risk management decisions, *Journal of Applied Corporate Finance*, Vol 15.1

Contingent capital is an "On demand" equity (Contingent Equity) or credit lines (LoC) that allows the firm to contain the paid up capital up to the risky event occurence;
This capital management tool boosts the company performances in reducing the equity requirement. The *contingent capital*, all insurances and derivatives are part of the *risk capital*.

Letters and Lines of Credit

Probably the most common example of a contingent debt claim is a letter or line of credit (LOC). In such an arrangement, a lender—usually a bank—accepts a fee from a corporation and in return agrees to lend the company money at a subsequent time of the corporation's choosing, provided the firm still meets certain criteria specified by the lender. If and when the corporation draws on the LOC, the contingent claim becomes an actual fixed claim in which the firm now owes interest and principal to the bank. LOCs may be either *committed or uncommitted*

Contingent Equity

A Contingent equity facility allows the user to issue new equity shares in exchange for cash if a triggering event occurs. This product represents a put option held by the equity issuer on its own common or preferred stock—and most contingent equity structures fall under the rubric of "loss equity puts." In a typical loss equity put, the firm essentially pre-negotiates and equity private placement with a single counterparty (or syndicate) in the form of an agreement that allows the firm to issue and sell new stock directly to the counterparty in the event a second trigger is activated (with the first trigger, again, being the firm's desire to issue new stock). The underlying may be preferred or common stock. If the stock is preferred, the dividend rate can be comparable to the rate paid on other preferred stock or it can be fixed.

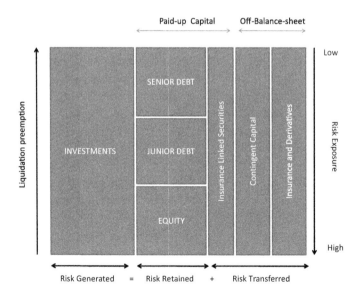

Figure 2.6: The Insurance Model with Off-Balance-Sheet Instruments and Contingent Capital.
Source: Shimpi (2001).

Besides the use of off-balance-sheet capital products, such as, financial derivatives and insurance contracts, the enterprise can activate another source of capital referred to as **contingent capital** (Cult, 2002; Conti, 2005; Doherty, 1995, 2005). Contingent capital is a capital management tool that enables a company to draw upon a reserve pool of money, providing protection from the financial ramifications of an unforeseen event, such as a natural disaster or severe market correction.

This financial source cannot be found on the enterprise balance sheet because it is activated by the occurrence of a loss and is made up of credit lines or capital sources that can be accessed on demand. Technically, these are forms of "knock-in" put options, or securities issued by the enterprise and issued by insurance companies and banks which are activated in case the threshold condition mentioned in the contract is violated. Use of contingent capital made of debt instruments do not provide a definitive transfer of risk, but rather a temporary one as the new credit lines activated will have to be repaid.

Emerging Market Example: Contingent Capital in Qatar and Saudi Arabia

Credit Suisse (CS) issued six billion Swiss francs of contingent convertible bonds (known as CoCos) and placed them with Qatar Holding, a sovereign wealth fund, and the Olayan Group, a Saudi conglomerate. This debt issue takes care of half of the contingent capital CS has to raise under a new Swiss law to strengthen the bank's balance sheets. The law takes effect in 2019.

The investors used the contingent convertible bonds to replace existing bonds in the portfolio of US$3.5 billion and 2.5 billion Swiss francs with coupons of 9.5% and 9% respectively. CoCos are like normal bonds except that they are converted into equity if a predetermined trigger event happens. In this case, the event would be a drop in the bank's Tier 1 capital ratio below 7%. The bonds are intended to bolster the bank's equity capital in a crisis situation.

Source: New York Times; February 2, 2011.

Contingent capital, insurance contracts and derivatives are part "venture capital" and constitute sources dedicated to the hedging of unanticipated risks.

The arguments presented so far were developed because they relate to the enterprise and are aimed at quantifying the relationship that exists between risk incurred and endowment capital of a stand-alone enterprise. The result is that these models do not include the possible effects of the risk diversification policies, which the borrowers can implement to reduce the specific risk of the enterprise. Assuming the investor's perspective and giving to the investor the possibility to diversify the specific risk incurred to invest in the enterprise, we can state that part of the risk retained by the lender can be reduced by resorting to diversification methods of the portfolio of investments we have seen in the section *"Risk Reduction, Diversification and Other Policies"*. In this third model, which includes the diversification of risk by the enterprise's lender, the relationship will be illustrated by the following:

Risk generated = Risk assets

= Risk retained after diversification

+ Risk transferred.

In this case, the risk retained after diversification will be smaller than the one previously carried due to the following relationship:

Risk retained − Risk diversified

= Risk retained after diversification.

In which:

Risk diversified = Risk retained − Risk retained

after diversification.

The risk retained by the enterprise after diversification decreases as a function of the independence of the results of the enterprise compared to those of the other investments placed in the asset portfolio of the lenders.

This situation is illustrated in Figure 2.7 in which diversification acts upon the specific risk borne both by shareholders and creditors, thus reducing it. In the presence of a solvent enterprise, however, that reduction will be only to the advantage of the shareholders.

All these considerations, which allow expanding the traditional considerations regarding the choices of the financing mix to maximize the value of the enterprise, highlight the importance of the adequacy of the endowment capital for the enterprise's existence. Before proceeding with a more detailed analysis of enterprise risk in its principal component, the financial

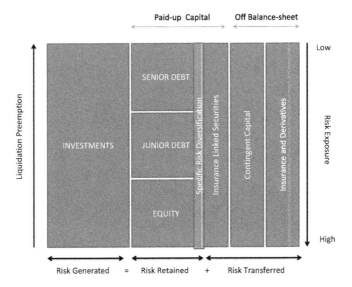

Figure 2.7:   The Risk Retained in the Insurance Model with Off-Balance-Sheet Instruments and Contingent Capital from the Perspective of the Diversified Risk Taker.
Source: Our chart.

structure risk, it is necessary to reflect on the relationship between risk generated by the company and its recipients (supplier of finance). This analysis anticipates the subjects discussed in the second part of this book.

Recipients of Enterprise Risk, Seniority and Insolvency

After this brief analysis of the extent of risk generated, its transferability to third-party recipients and magnitude of endowment capital, it is necessary to focus the analysis on the financial structure to understand how business and leverage risks are shared among the suppliers of finance (shareholders and bond/debts holders). The analysis will be performed in the case of enterprises with a financial structure characterized either by equity only or by debt and equity.

Before doing this, we want to start again from the concept of seniority and the hierarchy identified by law, regulations or individual covenants drawn up in the enterprise's financing instruments. We note that each financial instrument issued by the company can be ordered in accordance with the principle of preemption on cash flows. This is much more important when the cash flows generated by the enterprise are smaller.

In order to survive, the enterprise must generate enough cash flows to honor the commitments assumed for all lenders ranked according to the seniority: privileged creditors, unsecured creditors and finally shareholders. Privileged creditors include employees, professionals and craftsmen beside all creditors holding real or personal collateral. This category includes bondholders holding senior debt. Creditors backed by collaterals are, in fact, satisfied before the others in case of bankruptcy. With a lower seniority, we can quote creditors without guarantees or rights governed by law. These include bond creditors holding subordinated and/or mezzanine debt, and all non-commercial lenders and those not backed by guarantees. All of these creditors are satisfied only in case the request of privileged creditors is liquidated in full and there are remaining resources to distribute.

Company lenders are subject to different risk according to the capital structure defined by the management. Three potential capital structures are:

(1) The enterprise is financed entirely by equity;
(2) The enterprise is financed by equity and debt, and equity is sufficient compared to the MPL;
(3) The enterprise is financed by equity and debt and equity is sufficient compared to the net loss (for the year) and less than the MPL.

As seen in Table 2.5, in the first case the company and its suppliers of finance (the shareholders) hold operational risk only. In fact, the absence of other claimers make impossible the company bankruptcy due to financial risk but the risk is limited to business risk only.

In the second case, the shareholder holds business and leverage risk, and the lender the risk of default only. In the third case, where the endowment capital is lower than the MPL, the risks are being held by the shareholders up to the market value of the endowment capital. For the part of the loss exceeding the endowed capital the risk is transferred to the lenders.

Therefore, in order to understand what may happen to an enterprise having endowment capital sufficient or insufficient to cover the value of losses we need to relate the MPL to the distribution of enterprise potential earnings (Figure 2.8).

Let us suppose that we constructed the distribution of frequency of future enterprise earnings J. The expected result, in the event of a Gaussian distribution, is estimated at the mean value and will be equivalent to $\bar{R}_J$. In the event the enterprise obtains an actual yield greater than expected,

Table 2.5: Risk Takers in the Enterprise Financed by Equity and in the Enterprise Financed with Equity and Debt.

	HP	Shareholders	Lenders
Enterprise Financed with Equity alone	—	Business risk	—
Enterprise Financed with Equity and Debt with Endowment Capital **(Paid-up capital)** > MPL[12]	EC > MPL	Business and leverage risk	Insolvency risk zero
Enterprise Financed with Equity and Debt and with Net Loss (for the Year) Greater than EC and less than MPL	EC < NL < MPL	Business and leverage risk	Part business risk and leverage risk

Note: HP = Hypothesis.
EC = Paid-up capital or endowment capital.
MPL = Maximum Potential Loss.
NL = Net loss of the year.

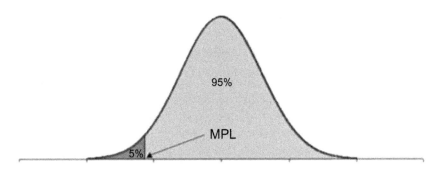

Figure 2.8: Distribution of Expected Earnings and MPL.
Source: Our formulation.

business leverage risks will be passed entirely to the shareholder. These risks will be retained by the shareholders even in the case when r_j is lower

---

[12]This case refers to a constant Equity > MPL situation. This does not rule out the occurrence of an actual loss greater than equity, but in the case under review it is assumed that the shareholder will recapitalize the enterprise in order to cover all or part of the loss, thus reconstituting capital stock. On the basis of this hypothesis, there is no possibility to generate a capital account loss for the bondholders, and so the insolvency risk is zero.

than $\bar{R}_J$ and greater than 0; or even in the case in which it is negative, at least until the following condition occurs:

Loss for the period $<$ market value of endowment capital

In fact, in the event loss exceeds endowment capital, a transfer of the risk to the bond holder will take place; the risk will be mainly financial in nature, but it may also originate from a negative event associated with operating activity.

This possibility justifies the request for a risk premium exceeding the risk free for lenders.

The normative consequence of what is just said is that management would lead endowment capital to be equal or greater than MPL, but this would not allow management to maximize the weighted average cost of capital (WACC) and consequently maximize enterprise value. Substantially, we must again choose a level of indebtedness whereby bankruptcy costs are minimized and enterprise value is maximized. The magnitude of the endowment capital will be optimal in this context, when the marginal cost of bankruptcy will be equal to the marginal benefit of the debt.

All this is stated in the absence of innovative policies in enterprise risk management. In fact, management could, using for instance the contingent capital, achieve the two objectives mentioned above at the same time.

He, substantially, would be determining equity on the basis of the ratio between costs and marginal benefits of the debt, but he may abate the expected risk not covered by it by using the contingent capital to be activated on the occasion of expected losses in excess of equity. However, what we have said so far does not allow the enterprise to be protected from the catastrophic effects of an unforeseen risk; for the reader's peace of mind we will point out that these instances are forecasted with a probability near zero.

The conclusion we draw from what has been stated thus far is that the economic or financial operation of an enterprise, reexamined from the standpoint of risk management principles, allows a management to manage risk actively to create value, and have the enterprise risk borne by shareholders and bond holders, who are adequately compensated for that risk.

Part 2

ESTIMATING DEFAULT RISK IN PRACTICE: METHODOLOGIES AND DISCRIMINANT VARIABLES

Chapter 3

CREDIT RISK, DEFAULT, AND BORROWING COSTS

Oliviero Roggi and Alessandro Giannozzi

Definition of Default/Credit Risk from the Perspective of the Bank

"The risk of any loan is the probability that the transaction will not contribute in a positive sense to the financial company's profitability, or it could have a negative impact on the operating income". In 1965, Dell' Amore[1] illustrated that credit risk was directly tied to the borrower's ability to provide remuneration on the loan obtained and repayment of the principal. More recently, credit risk was defined by Sironi (2000) as "the eventuality that an unexpected change in credit rating might occur, which could generate a sudden change in the market value of the lending position".[2]

Both these cited definitions contain the two fundamental elements of credit risk:

(a) The risk of default, defined as the probability that the enterprise is not able to pay interest on the debt and repay the principal lent;
(b) The migration risk related to the deterioration of the enterprise's credit rating.

---

[1]Dell' Amore (1965).
[2]See Sironi (2000).

The first element of risk is not unique given that the deterioration of a credit rating can generate a reduction in the market value of debt exposure. An example is a bond "listed" in regulated markets that has been assigned a specific rating, by an external agency. From the standpoint of the risk-return approach, any downgrading[3] resulting from the deterioration of the issuer's credit quality would result in an increase in the default spread required by investors. Since it is not possible to change the nominal rate of the bond, this downgrading will result in a reduction in the market price of the security listed. In reality, **migration risk**, which is also defined as **spread risk**, is not only connected with the possibility of migrating from one rating category to another, but can also result from general market conditions. It is possible that the "market", or more precisely investors, may request an increase in the rate differential relative to risk free securities for bonds belonging to the same rating category. This phenomenon is based on the existing relationship between investors' risk aversion, the premium for risk and economic conditions of financial markets and not on the enterprise's credit rating.

Migration risk not only concerns bonds, but also the lending relationships that the bank establishes with its borrowing customers.[4]

At the operational level, the measurement of credit risk requires the quantification of two components[5]: expected loss (EL) and unexpected loss (UL).[6] EL represents the loss that the intermediary expects in relation to a loan position, while the latter is an expression, in terms of variability, of the referenced value.[7]

---

[3] In the technical language of rating agencies, downgrading is defined as the downgrade of enterprise creditworthiness to a lower category of rating assigned to the asset, e.g., from BBB to BB.

[4] One of the goals of Basel II is to evaluate the borrower not only at the time of the credit facility request, but also during the life of the loan. By doing so, any deterioration or improvement in credit quality will be directly reflected in the provision of capital for regulatory purposes, and as a result, in the interest rate applied to the transaction concerned.

[5] See Saunders and Allen (2002).

[6] The New Capital Accord (NCA) is structured to provide coverage for both the EL and UL components. This differs from the models used by banks up until now that specify that the EL must be covered by an appropriate provision, while UL must be covered by capital for regulatory purposes. In essence, the NCA also extends capital coverage to the EL component. However, in reality EL is taken into account in determining the loan's interest rate.

[7] See Saunders and Allen (2002); Van Gestel and Baesens (2009); De Servigny and Renault (2004).

Given the characteristics of the borrower, the amount of the EL determines the loan's pricing, when providing a credit facility.

About 20 years ago, banks focused almost exclusively on estimating EL without worrying about the possibility that the actual loss could, *a posteriori*, be greater than the ELs. On the other hand, the evolution of studies on banking "shifted" the focus to the UL.

The distinction between EL and UL is essential from an accounting standpoint with respect to the former; the bank must adjust the value of the asset or recognize a risk provision in the income statement, while the latter will be covered out by bank's capital. The bank's shareholders are able to benefit from operating profits that exceed expectations when actual losses are lower than those estimated, while they incur a charge resulting from any realized losses greater than expected.

In the following paragraphs, the components of EL and the relationship between it and the cost of borrowing for the enterprise are analyzed from a corporate perspective. The problems of estimating UL, and value at risk (VaR),[8] represent one of the major areas of research for credit risk management scholars, who address this issue from the bank's perspective.

Components of Credit Risk

Estimating EL

At the time of default, the EL of a credit exposure is a function of two factors[9]:

— The value of the credit exposure expected at the time of default [exposure at default (EAD)];
— The EL rate attributable to such credit exposure [expected loss rate (ELR)].

---

[8]VaR is a statistical method for measuring risk and is able to summarize the risk for the entire portfolio in a single number. It represents the maximum expected risk for a given exposure or a given portfolio over a given time horizon within the limits of a specific confidence interval.

From a technical standpoint, it is calculated as the difference between the expected value of the probability distribution of future losses (expression of EL) and the maximum probable value associated with a certain confidence level (given by an appropriate percentage). This technique is based on a methodology for controlling market risk developed by JP Morgan in the 1990s.

[9]See Resti and Sironi (2007); De Servigny and Renault (2004).

In turn, ELR is defined as the product of two additional factors:

— The probability of the borrower's default [probability of default (PD)];
— The expected amount of the non-recoverable portion of the loan in the event of default [loss given default (LGD)].

To formalize this relationship, EL, expressed as an absolute value, is the product of EAD, the PD and the LGD.

$$EL = EAD * PD * LGD.$$

I will analyze the theoretical and practical aspects involved in the measurement of the credit risk components as follows.

Calculation of EAD

The estimation of EAD is based on the following elements:

(1) The current utilized portion of the credit facility [defined as the drawn portion (DP)];
(2) The unutilized portion at the time of valuation [undrawn portion (UP)];
(3) The percentage of the unutilized portion expected to be used by the borrower at the time of default [usage given default (UGD)].[10]

When estimating EAD, it is essential to take into account the unutilized portion of the credit facility and project what portion of it will be used by the enterprise at the time of default. When getting close to default, enterprises tend to increase exposure up to the limits of the credit facility provided by the bank to cover financial imbalances that are occurring.[11] As a result, the amount of the credit facility used by a healthy enterprise and EAD can differ significantly. This is why the above indicators have such an important indicative function.

The formula for determining the proper exposure for the unutilized portion of the credit facility is as follows:

$$EAD = DP + UP * UGD.$$

At this point it is essential to cover an important aspect connected with estimating EAD. The unutilized portion of the credit facility is taken into account and will inevitably result in an increase in EL, which in theory

---

[10]See Smithson (2003).
[11]See Ong (1999).

should lead to an increase in the price of borrowing for the enterprise. In other words, the greater loss perceived by the lender will result in an increase in the **spread** applied to the enterprise to compensate the bank for the greater risk incurred, which in this case is implicit in the unutilized portion. However, in most cases this risk component is covered by a fee widely used in Anglo–Saxon markets called the "commitment fee".[12]

The estimate of the PD

The second EL factor consists of the entity's PD, which represents the probability of the occurence of an "insolvency" event. The determination of this probability implies the assessment of a statistical model for projecting insolvencies. Using mathematical and statistical techniques (Altman, 1968, 1977, 2000; Ohlson, 1980; Blum, 1974; Zmijewski, 1984; Altman, Giannozzi, Sabato and Roggi, 2013; Roggi and Giannozzi, 2009), it is possible to assign an *ex-ante* estimate of the PD to each borrower. Prior to calculating the PD, it is necessary to identify the event that will serve as a proxy for default.[13] In the following paragraphs of this chapter, we will cover the various default concepts used in empirical research on risk of default and in operational practice in banks.

Another aspect to be determined prior to creating the statistical model is the determination of the time horizon of the assessments, i.e., the value over time of insolvency projections. The basis for estimating the forecasting model is derived from the time lag for collecting the learning sample.[14] The reference time projection must not be of a short duration,[15] and in any event, must be related to the duration of the credit relationship.[16] It is a well-established practice in both the ratings of specialized agencies and in

---

[12] "*Massimo scoperto* (maximum credit limit)" is used to indicate the high point in the customer's borrowings in the relationship between the bank and the customer. It is taken into account in all time periods for the determination of interest to be charged to the customer. In fact, the bank applies a percentage fee to the maximum credit limit which is charged to the customer. Decree Law No. 223 of July 4, 2006, which was converted to Law No. 248 on August 4, 2006, declared the maximum credit limit fee to be null and void.

[13] See De Laurentis, Maino and Molteni (2010).

[14] The learning sample is the database used to assess the default prediction model.

[15] Assessments of the insolvency risk of counterparties based on short periods may result in an inappropriate assessment of significant conditions, which form the basis of the assessment of the prompt fulfillment of the financial obligations by the borrowing counterparty.

[16] According to Bank of Italy, banks will estimate PD over a time horizon of a year. In this connection.

banking and academic practice to determine the one-year PD. This time period is consistent with bank credit facility procedures, which call for an annual review of credit facilities.

Probabilities can be aggregated by risk category in order to determine a rating.[17] The bank must first determine the two categories at the extremes of the rating scale: the "best" rating, which includes enterprises with the highest credit standing with a very low default risk (PD) estimated, and the "worst" rating category, which includes enterprises at which a default[18] will occur. The bank must determine the number of categories to be placed on the rating scale and the size of each category.[19] These decisions will not be covered in depth in this book since they constitute problems that are typically of a banking nature. However, it is understandable that these decisions can have an impact on the enterprise's assessment, and in particular, on its borrowing cost.

Estimation of LGD

The last parameter to be estimated for the calculation of EL, is the LGD.

The following formula can be used to express this parameter as a percentage:

$$LGD = 1 - RR,$$

where

LGD = portion of the loan that banks will not recover in the event of default;
RR (recovery rate) = the loan recovery rate.

In essence, while the PD of a borrower depends on the specific credit rating, and thus, on the current and future operating and financial conditions of the enterprise. The LGD reflects the unique characteristics of the lending transaction.

---

[17]To build a rating model, see Lando (2004); De Laurentis, Maino and Molteni (2010); Wilson (1997a, 1997b); Saunders (1997).
[18]Here default is not estimated, but reported: these are enterprises in which a default has occurred.
[19]A PD range will correspond to each rating category. The "durability" of a rating model must be tested after the fact by identifying the frequency of defaults found in each category and checking whether these are consistent with the probability interval, determined *ex-ante*.

The LGD component is a function of the following factors[20]:

1. The type of lending transaction used.
2. The existence of collateral supporting the credit facility.
3. The value of the collateral compared to the debt exposure of the customer.
4. The ability to convert the aforementioned collateral into cash, and the time profile for doing so.
5. The timing and costs of recovery.

The recovery rate[21] of the loan exposure will be determined as the ratio of the net amount recovered to the exposure at the time of default. Specifically, the recovery rate can be expressed as follows:

$$\text{recovery rate} = \frac{\sum_{t=1}^{t=n} \frac{\text{Val}R_t}{(1+i)^t} - \sum_{t=1}^{t=n} \frac{\text{Val}S_t}{(1+i)^t}}{\text{EAD}}, \qquad (1)$$

where

$\text{Val}R$ = amounts recovered over the period from $t = 1$ to $t = n$.
$\text{Val}S$ = expenses incurred for the recovery over the period from $t = 1$ to $t = n$.
EAD = exposure at the time of default.
i = discount rate.

Specifically, this will involve estimating the amounts recovered, the amount of expenses incurred for the recovery and the time distribution. These factors depend on the value of the "collateral base" and the ability to convert the latter to cash. Since these amounts are distributed over time, they must be "discounted" using the rate i[22] to account for the time value of money.

The LGD is dependent upon the recovery rate, the type and value of the "collateral base" and the type and form of transaction.[23] Based on the

---

[20]In this regard, see Van Gestel and Baesens (2009).
[21]See De Servigny and Renault (2004).
[22]The discount rate must express the marginal cost of funding for the bank, and is usually estimated by using an interbank rate.
[23]It is understood that there are specific loan agreements in which the bank may easily draw on collateral, and others in which recovery requires incurring significant expenses and long periods of time.

above criteria, a reduction in the LGD on a general level could be obtained by reducing the drawing periods for the recovery of the loans in default.[24]

Methods for estimating recovery rates

A feasible way of doing this is the use of the **bank's internal estimate.** This estimate is made on the basis of **historical experience** with its loan portfolio. In this case, the loan portfolio is segmented by borrower category, type of exposure and collateral provided in order to estimate average historical recovery rates.

In this assessment process, the bank must see the recovery rate in a financial sense, and not just an accounting sense, and actually estimate the present value of resources from the various phases in the recovery process up until the end of the dispute. In addition, it is necessary to take into account certain variables such as:

(a) The percentage of loans that are projected to be recovered as a function of both the form of loan and the collateral provided (ER).
(b) External administrative costs that the bank must incur, such as legal costs, and internal costs for staff in charge of recoveries and for any areas dedicated to the recovery process (AC).
(c) The recovery period, which is derived from the execution procedure used (t).
(d) The rate used to discount expected recoveries, which is generally the same as the interbank rate (i).

The Relationship between EL and Borrowing Cost: Loan Pricing

Segregating enterprises into rating categories, each with a related value for expected loss, makes it possible to calculate an initial specification for risk adjusted pricing.[25] This process makes it possible to formulate policies for differentiating loan interest rates based on the related credit risk.[26]

By making the amount of two investments with an equal unit value; the first being a risk free investment, and the second having an interest

---

[24]With regard to the costs and timing of recoveries, see Generale and Gobbi (1996).
[25]With regard to the methodologies used to set loan interest rates, see Saunders and Allen (2002).
[26]These are indicators that do not require specifications of VaR models or the quantification of the portfolio effect by assessing correlations among borrowers. This approach is used to set pricing which is only a function of the EL.

rate of i_p which only applies to the portion of principal lent and does not generate losses, we arrive at the following equation:

$$(1 - \text{ELR}) \cdot (1 + i_p) = 1 + i_{rf}, \tag{2}$$

where

ELR = expected loss rate.
i_{rf} = risk-free interest rate.

This simple pricing model is constructed taking into account the fact that the bank is able to obtain the rate required, only on the portion of the loan that does not generate losses.

Looking more closely at the previous equation for the interest rate to be applied to the loan we get:

$$i_p = \frac{i_{rf} + \text{ELR}}{1 - \text{ELR}}, \tag{3}$$

$$i_p = \frac{i_{rf} + \text{PD} \cdot \text{LGD}}{1 - \text{PD} \cdot \text{LGD}}. \tag{4}$$

The latter formula estimates loan pricing for amounts greater than the sum of the risk-free and EL (the denominator is less than 1), based on the fact that this rate can be obtained only on the portion of the loan that does not generate a loss,[27] i.e., $(1 - \text{ELR})$.

The same equation shows that the interest rate that enterprises will have to pay to obtain a loan tends to rise as a function of ELs, i.e., as a function of PD and LGD. This relationship between pricing and EL can be shown by analyzing the **Credit Spread**:

$$i_p - i_{rf} = \frac{\text{PD} \cdot \text{LGD} \cdot (1 + i_{rf})}{1 - \text{PD} \cdot \text{LGD}}. \tag{5}$$

The above formula shows that the borrowing cost of an enterprise depends on the PD of such enterprise. The latter, in turn, depends on the current and future operating and financial condition and on the LGD. Thus, the lower the LGD, the lower the premium for risk that the enterprise will have to pay to the bank.

In order to complete the pricing relationship covered to this point, it is necessary to remove the assumption of equality with the risk-free and also

---

[27]See Ghosh (2012); Saunders and Allen (2002); McAllister and Mingo (1994); Wilson (1997a, 1997b); Saunders (1997).

consider the equity risk premium asked by bank's stockholders.[28] In this case, the relationship

$$(1 - \text{ELR}) \cdot (1 + i_p) = 1 + i_{rf}, \tag{6}$$

is structured as follows:

$$1 + i_{rf} + i_k = (1 - \text{PD}) \cdot (1 + i_p) + \text{PD} \cdot (1 - \text{LGD}) \cdot (1 + i_p). \tag{7}$$

The Estimate of UL and VaR: Outline

If we take the bank's perspective in estimating the risk of the credit portfolio, it is necessary to take another parameter into consideration: UL,[29] which represents a measure of the degree of dispersion of the loss rate around its mean value.[30] The well-known statistical concepts of variance and standard deviation can be used to measure this parameter. If, for example, one assumes that for a given loan position, n scenarios can be observed in relation to which the loss rate (LR) varies according to a probability distribution, the measure of the dispersion of the LR can be expressed as follows:

$$\sigma = \sqrt{\sum_{i=1}^{n} \frac{[\text{LR}_i - E(\text{LR})]^2}{n - 1}}, \tag{8}$$

where

LR = actual loss rate.

E(LR) = expected loss rate.

Thus, we can see that the risk that generates a loss greater than the expected loss is higher, higher the level of dispersion of loss rates around the mean.

Therefore, the UL is tied to the possibility that at the maturity of a loan provided, the loss actually incurred may be greater than the estimated loss as a result of possible errors made *a priori* in estimating the PD and LGD. For additional details on models that estimate UL, see Lando (2004).

The concept of UL leads to another risk measurement tool which was developed by JP Morgan in the 1990s and is widely used in banking practice

---

[28]It is obvious that a shareholder investing in the bank assumes enterprise risk, and thus, must be compensated with an appropriate premium for such risk. This makes it necessary, in the loan pricing procedure, to also consider the return expected by shareholders.
[29]This risk must be covered by the bank's capital. See Saita (2007); Schroeck (2002).
[30]See Lando (2004).

to estimate the maximum EL on a portfolio of exposures: VaR. This represents the maximum expected risk for a given exposure or a given portfolio over a given time horizon within the limits of a specific confidence interval. From a technical standpoint, it is calculated as the difference between the expected value of the probability distribution of future losses (expression of EL) and the maximum probable value associated with a certain confidence level (given by an appropriate percentage).[31]

The bank needs the VaR estimate in order to determine the "capital at risk" to be set aside to cover any losses.

Leading scholars in the area of banking risk management indicate that one of the main problems associated with estimating VaR concerns the asymmetrical nature of the distribution of losses connected with credit risk.[32] One type of distribution that can approximate the asymmetrical trend is the "beta distribution",[33] which is characterized by two parameters, α and β, which define the "height" and kurtosis of distribution respectively. It is intuitive that a good credit rating of an enterprise makes the asymmetry more pronounced reflecting the low probability of incurring high losses. On the other hand, low credit quality corresponds to an ELR distribution trending toward normality with a sharp reduction in asymmetry. Using μ to indicate the EL corresponding to a rating category and maturity of the individual exposure $(\mathrm{EL}_{j,t})$, and σ to indicate the standard deviation related to the unexpected loss rate $(\mathrm{ULR}_{j,t})$, it is possible to determine VaR, or capital at risk, as the inverse of the "beta function" at the confidence level selected. The mean and variance are as follows:

$$\mu = \frac{\alpha}{\alpha + \beta} \quad \sigma^2 = \frac{\alpha \cdot \beta}{(\alpha + \beta)^2 \cdot (\alpha + \beta + 1)}, \tag{9}$$

---

[31]This technique is based on a methodology for controlling market risk developed by JP Morgan in the 1990s.

[32]For example, credit risk is characterized by behavior that is completely different from market risk. In fact, the probability of a market rise or decline should be the same under conditions of efficiency and liquidity. It can be inferred that market risk can be represented by a distribution similar to a Gaussian distribution, and thus, with gains and losses distributed symmetrically *vis-à-vis* the expected value, which is equal to 0, but with thicker tails due to the higher probability of the manifestation of the extreme positive and negative events (see Figure 3.1).

For credit risk, the situation is quite different, since in this case, it is not possible to generate a gain. Thus, under the best circumstances, this risk can generate a loss of zero. When insolvencies of borrowers occur, losses start generating up to the point of the potential elimination of the nominal value of the loans made. In fact, it is impossible to represent credit risk with a symmetrical, or normal, distribution.

[33]In "beta distribution", the lower the mean value, the higher is asymmetry.

Risk, Value and Default

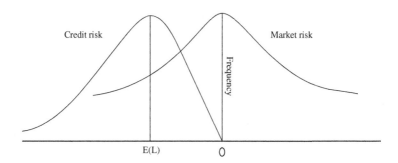

Figure 3.1: Distribution of Density of Market Risk and Credit Risk.

from which

$$\alpha = \frac{\mu \cdot (\mu - \mu^2 - \sigma^2)}{\sigma^2} \mathrm{e}, \quad \beta = \frac{\dfrac{(1 - \mu) \cdot \mu^2 + (\mu \cdot \sigma^2)}{\sigma^2 \cdot (1 - \mu)}}{\mu}. \tag{10}$$

From the bank's standpoint, it will be necessary to move from a specific, individual VaR for an exposure, to a diversified, or marginal, VaR. The latter will definitely be lower than the former since a part of the credit risk of the individual loan is reduced by the diversification of the loan portfolio. In this work, we have decided to leave out a detailed analysis of problems associated with estimating the VaR of a portfolio since that research area falls under banking-related subjects.

The Enterprise and the "Challenge" of Basel II as an External Stimulus for Risk Measurement

New Concepts Introduced by Basel II

In many countries lending activities have seen growing levels of risk as evidenced by the recurrence of numerous significant bank crises starting in the 1970s.

As a result of the opening of financial markets, the growing volatility of interest and exchange rates and more intense competition, generated a high ratio of non-performing loans to capital for banks, and thus, indirectly resulted in a heightened focus on risk-related problems.

In particular, market globalization along with the widespread process of deregulation accelerated the growth in demand for financial services and competitive pressures on the other side (new intermediaries, new forms of intermediation and new markets) thereby changing risk profiles. The latter have become more complex, interconnected and difficult to diversify.

Changes in the environment pointed toward the need for developing "safeguards" to protect the stability of the monetary and financial system.

For banking intermediaries this involved a gradual abandonment by regulatory authorities with the approach based on "direct controls" (lending limits, portfolio restrictions, etc.) in favor of a new paradigm based on the need to force banking operations to comply with precise ratios between "risks assumed/managed" and the related "capital endowment".

Against this background, the First Basel Accord on Bank Capital (1988) was introduced under the name Basel I.

Based on the fundamental principle of the Basel accords: *"all assets created by banks involve the assumption of a risk to be quantified and supported with capital, which is also called regulatory capital"*.

In 1988, the Basel Committee[34] introduced the following concept of *"Capital Adequacy for Banks"*:

$$\frac{\text{PV}}{\text{risk-weighted assets}} \geq 8\%,$$

where $\text{PV} = $ capital for regulatory purposes.[35]

---

[34] The Basel Committee is an advisory body established by the governors of the central banks of the ten most industrialized countries (G10) at the end of 1974. The aim of the Committee is to promote cooperation between central banks and other equivalent agencies in order to ensure the monetary and financial stability of the lending system. It has no supranational authority, and its conclusions have no legal force. The guidelines, standards and recommendations of the Committee are formulated with the expectation that individual national authorities will be able to draft operating provisions that take into account the situation in individual countries. In this way, the Committee encourages convergence toward common approaches and standards.

[35] Capital for regulatory purposes is the sum of Tier 1 capital (included in the calculation without limitations) and Tier 2 capital (included up to the limit in the amount of Tier 1 capital). Tier 1 capital — included without limitations: (+) share capital, (+) reserves, (+) reserve for general banking risks, (−) goodwill, (−) treasury stock, (−) intangible assets, (−) current and past losses. Tier 2 capital — included up to the amount of Tier 1 capital: (+) revaluation reserves, (+) subordinated liabilities, (+) allowance for doubtful debt (+/−) net capital gains or losses on equity investments).

Certain elements are deducted from the sum of Tier 1 and Tier 2 such as: equity investments in credit institutions and financial equity investments greater than 10% of the share capital of the subsidiary or affiliate; equity investments less than 10%, which are deducted only to the extent they exceed 10% of the value of Tier 1 and Tier 2 capital.

In other words, the capital to be considered for regulatory purposes must be in proportion to the volume and risk of loans ("risk assets"), which is reflected in weighting coefficients that differ as a function of the nature of the entity (sovereign states, government agencies, credit facilities to individuals, etc.). In particular, the weighting coefficient for credit facilities provided to enterprises was 100% regardless of the credit rating of the individual entities. This means that for a loan of 100 euros provided to an enterprise, the bank will have a capital requirement of 8 euros regardless of whether the borrower is of excellent quality or has solvency problems.

In this context, capital requirements were based on a simple rule that could be immediately applied, and they played an essential role in stimulating the growth of bank capitalization and the enhancement of capital strength. However, both the banking industry and the world of scientific research realized that this risk assessment rule was too simplistic.

In fact, the rigid weighting coefficients did not take into account the actual quality of an asset in the financial statements or a loan, the term of the loan or instruments used to mitigate risks (collateral and guarantees, credit derivatives, the securitization of loan rights, etc.). As a result, the quantity of capital absorbed was not very sensitive to the actual credit risk of the counterparties.

Within this operating framework, moral hazard phenomena occurred in which banks preferred to make loans to highly risky entities in order to obtain high interest rates, and thus, greater profits. In fact, this behavior did not impair the ability to expand operations: the capital absorbed remained the same even if loans were made to highly risky enterprises.

In the context of Base I, there was a "mispricing"[36] of loans since customers with a high credit standing paid interest rates that were higher than their individual risk, while customers with a low credit standing enjoyed interest rates lower than they deserved in relation to their risk. This situation was primarily dictated by the lack of accurate methodologies for assessing credit standings and by the pursuit of strategies that mainly focused on loan growth. In addition, on an average, there has been an

---

[36]The author uses "mispricing" to mean an incorrect determination of loan pricing. He also talks about a "cross subsidy" in which segments of customers with a high risk of insolvency enjoyed interest rates which were lower than those that should have been applied in proportion to their risk, while higher quality customers paid higher interest rates than their credit rating would dictate.

"underpricing" of loans relative to the average risk of the loan portfolio of banks, and this is not consistent with the goal of maximizing the value of the banking enterprise.

It was on the very basis of the limits of this agreement that the banking system perceived the need to improve the quality of financial statement assets and to "price" loans to properly reflect the credit risk to which the bank is exposed.

In 2001 and again in 2003,[37] the Basel Committee prepared a provisional document called the **NCA**[38] and revised the capital ratio by establishing new "weightings" which are assigned to each loan, on the basis of the credit standing of the borrower measured in the form of an alphanumeric opinion, or rating. The final version of this accord was made public in June 2004.[39] Basel II is formed around three mutually reinforcing pillars:

— *Minimum Capital Requirements*: Describes in detail the criteria and methodologies for measuring credit risks, market risks and operational risks[40] from which the quantification is derived for capital requirements that the banks are required to comply with.

— *Supervisory Review*: Specifies the role of the regulatory authorities. The latter are required to continually monitor the adequacy of capitalization in relation to risks and to assess the consistency of management policies implemented by banks to comply with the ratios set by the regulation. The Committee established new rules concerning the supervisory activities performed by regulatory authorities with respect to the suitability of capital requirements, and gave these authorities the power to validate internal processes that individual banks will implement in order to assess the credit risk of borrowers and other types of risk.

— *Market Discipline*: Introduces information and reporting obligations, i.e., disclosure requirements. In particular, it asks banks to provide the market with information that allows shareholders, investors and

---

[37]In 2001, a provisional document was prepared which was then revised in April 2003.

[38]See Basel Committee (2001). In April 2003, the committee prepared a document with certain revisions to the 2001 document.

[39]Basel Committee on Banking Supervision (2004).

[40]The existence of capital requirements to cover operational risks is a new aspect of the NCA since the 1988 Accord did not specify any coverage for this risk category.

savers to know the true risk profiles and capitalization levels of a bank in order to assess its strength.[41]

Basel II, for the first time, introduces a distinction between levels of capital absorption as a function of credit standing. This approach does not modify the capital adequacy coefficient of banks, which was introduced under Basel I and will continue to apply for regulatory purposes (8%), nor does it modify the procedures for calculating the numerator, i.e., capital for regulatory purposes. It does, however, change the method for determining the weighting coefficient in the denominator of the ratio.

$$\text{Risk asset ratio} = \frac{C}{A + [(M + O) * 12.5]} \geq 8\%,$$

where

A = assets weighted for credit risk
M = capital requirements to cover market risks
O = capital requirements to cover operational risk
C = capital for regulatory purposes

In addition, Basel II allows banks to use risk assessment methodologies that are increasingly complex in the hope that the adoption of more sophisticated solutions will lead to benefits in terms of lower capital absorption. In particular, two possible alternatives are introduced for determining capital coefficients connected with risk assets: the Standardized Approach and the Internal Rating Based (IRB) Approach. The latter is broken down into two types: Foundation and Advanced.

Measurement of Credit Risk in Accordance with Basel II Standardized Approach and IRB Approach

The Standardized Approach differentiates the weighting of risks of individual credit positions as a function of external ratings[42] assigned by

---

[41]It is obvious that the prudential approach is consistent with allocation decisions of shareholders, investors and markets, aimed at increasing the return on capital.

[42]For many small and medium-sized enterprises (SMEs), the costs of obtaining a rating from specialized agencies are exorbitant. As a result, the Basel Committee has specified that these enterprises will be considered among "retail" customers when the exposure to any SME is not greater than one million euros, and the exposure to any single borrower does not exceed 0.2% of the overall exposure of the "retail" portfolio. The SMEs meeting these parameters will not have to obtain a rating, and will be assigned a more favorable weighting of 75%.

Table 3.1: Weighting Coefficients in the Standardized Approach.

S&P Rating	AAA to AA−	A+ to A−	BBB+ to BBB−	Under BBB−	No rating
Risk Weighting	20%	50%	100%	150%	100%

recognized agencies,[43] and calls for the following coefficients for credit facilities provided to enterprises (see Table 3.1).

It should be noted that with the introduction of the Standardized Approach, loans to enterprises with a rating ≤ BBB− have a weighting factor of 150%. In percentage terms, these enterprises will require a provision of 12% of the amount of the credit facility.

An enterprise with a rating of A+ (50% weighting) will allow the bank to set aside less than what was required under Basel I. Thus, capital for regulatory purposes will be equal to 4% of loans.

In the IRB Approach, capital for regulatory purposes is calculated as a function of the projection of the degree of risk of the enterprise/borrower by using internal rating models.[44] In this case, weighting coefficients will be a continual function of the rating, and not a discrete function as in the case of the Standardized Approach.

---

[43]The rating made by specialized agencies must meet the requirements of objectivity, independence, transparency and disclosure of transactions. At the same time, agencies must have suitable organizational resources and reliable procedures for determining the rating.
[44]The NCA specifies that banks that use the IRB Approach must estimate and apply rating models for all the various "sub-portfolios" of the bank's assets. In practice, four types of models will be required for:

• Enterprises, sovereign states, banks and government entities.
• "Retail" product lines.
• Specialized lending.
• Equity investments.

With regard to the "boundaries" between corporate and retail, the NCA specifies that the corporate portfolio includes enterprises with revenues over 50 million euros, those with revenues of between 5–50 million euros and those with revenues under five million euros with exposure of over one million euros. All companies that fall under the corporate portfolio must be assessed individually using ratings. All enterprises that do not meet these parameters are considered "retail", and for them the NCA specifies that banks may estimate risk components (probability of bankruptcy and LGD) for every pool of exposures rather than for each individual borrower.

Internal ratings serve the function of translating all significant available information on a borrower into a summary opinion which is broken down into various rating categories.

To calculate risk weighting coefficients, banks that use the IRB Approach must determine the following four components of EL for each loan position:

— PD of the borrower.
— LGD, which, as noted in the above paragraphs, depends on the type of loan, and the type and degree of liquidity of collateral and guarantees obtained to support the loan.[45]
— EAD, which depends on the type of credit transaction.
— Effective maturity[46] of existing exposure, which depends on the loan type.

As stated above, the Basel Committee established two methods for the IRB Approach: the IRB Foundation Approach and the IRB Advanced Approach. Basically, banks that use the Foundation Approach independently estimate the PD and use bank regulatory criteria for the other three components of risk. On the other hand, credit institutions that use the Advanced Approach, rely on their own estimates of all four components to calculate risk weightings (see Table 3.2).

Basel II implicitly created an incentive for using the IRB Approach which would imply, all other conditions being equal, lower capital absorption than under Basel I. This should indirectly result in better "pricing" for "high-quality" enterprises. We will cover this topic in the following paragraph.

---

[45]The LR also depends on the type of procedure used for managing disputes (geographic location), the estimate of possible recovery costs, discount rate the trading cost of the position and the legal system used for the protection of the loan.

[46]The concept of maturity refers to the financial term of a loan, and can be defined as follows:

$$\text{maturity} = \frac{\sum_t t \cdot \text{CF}_t}{\sum_t \text{CF}_t}, \tag{11}$$

where

CF_t = total cash flows (interest and principal) that the borrower is required to pay in periods t;
$t \ (1, 2, 3, \ldots, T)$ = periods when payments are made.

Table 3.2:   Credit Risk Components and Estimation Methods in Accordance with Basel II.

Risk Parameters	Foundation Approach	Advanced Approach
PD	Internal rating system (IRS)	IRS
EAD	Parameters set by Committee	To be estimated using the internal model
LGD	Parameters set by Committee	To be estimated using the internal model
Maturity	Parameters set by Committee	To be calculated[47]

Source: Our calculations.

The Impact of Basel II on the Loans Pricing for Enterprises

With Basel II, banks' capital requirements depend on the rating of loans, and hence loan pricing should be more exact since it is a function of the rating and capital absorbed by the credit facility.[48]

In general, based on this, it should be possible to arrive at more exact loan pricing which would entail a reduction in borrowing cost for customers with a high credit standing and an increase in interest expense[49] for customers with a low credit standing. The capital requirement that banks should maintain for customers with a low rating is much higher than under the 1988 Accord. Furthermore, the internal ratings system is capable of more precisely determining the credit risk of borrowers and the related capital to be maintained than in the past.

Another aspect that has a significant impact on the amount of capital absorbed by the loan, and thus on the borrowing cost for the enterprise, is the role played by collateral.[50] These are instruments capable of mitigating the credit risk to which the bank is exposed, and thus, if recognized by the

---

[47]Banks that use the Advanced IRB Approach are required to measure the effective maturity of each transaction. However, effective maturity must be the greater of a year or the actual remaining life expressed in years. Effective maturity may not, in any case, be greater than five years.
[48]According to the 1988 Accord, the weighting coefficient for loans made to enterprises was always equal to 1 regardless of the credit standing of the entity. With the advent of the NCA, the riskiest credit facilities will absorb more capital, and thus, the rates applied to them will be higher than in the past. The reason for this is to maximize the return for the bank's shareholders.
[49]See Saunders and Allen (2002).
[50]In this regard, see Ayadi and Resti (2004).

NCA, could reduce the capital requirements for the loan, and therefore also reduce rates applied to customers.

Under the NCA, the weighting coefficients to be applied to loans to determine capital requirements is a function of the PD identified by the rating, and of the LGD, which is closely tied to the collateral provided by the borrower and the remaining maturity of the loan. Therefore, collateral have an impact on the "LGD" variable by reducing the loss in the event of insolvency and, as a result, mitigating the risk connected with exposure and the necessary capital requirements. Once the weighting coefficient has been determined on the basis of the above parameters, it is applied to exposure, in order to obtain a risk-weighted asset (RWA), which serves as the denominator in the capital ratio.[51]

The 1988 Accord allows for capital reductions for a limited number of guarantees [guarantees of countries or banks of the Organisation for Economic Co-operation and Development (OECD)] and financial collateral.[52] The NCA significantly broadens the variety of techniques and tools that can be used to mitigate risk[53] with additional categories of guarantees and collateral and expands the range of guarantors. In broadening the set of tools, the ability of credit derivatives[54] to reduce risk is specifically recognized, and where allowed by local bankruptcy laws, it is possible to offset loans against deposits in the financial statements. This is a set of highly significant innovations since the broader and more structured recognition of these mitigating instruments has an impact on capital requirements that captures the interest of the entire banking community. In terms of collateral (collateral security on financial assets), there are two approaches[55]: the simple approach, which can be used as a part of the Standardized Approach, and the overall approach (called the Comprehensive Approach in the NCA), which will allow banks that use the more advanced approach to use internal models[56] to estimate the mitigating effect of various guarantees. With regard to the simple approach, the following types of security

---

[51]See Saita (2007).
[52]These are financial instruments recognized as loan guarantees. See Basel Committee (1988).
[53]In this regard, see Murphy (2008).
[54]These financial instruments make it possible to assess and consequently transfer the implicit credit risk in credit exposure.
[55]See Basel Committee (2003); Basel Committee on Banking Supervision (2004).
[56]These are models based on historical observations of the appropriate strength of the mitigating effect of the various guarantees, and such models must be validated by regulatory authorities.

are recognized for financial assets: deposits, certificates of deposit, gold, stocks listed in major indices, certain types of shares or mutual funds, bonds issued by countries with a rating of at least BB− and bonds issued by other entities with a rating of at least BBB−; shares that are not listed in a major index, but that are traded in a recognized market are added for the Comprehensive Approach.

The part of the NCA concerning security is definitely significant for enterprises as well since by using advanced hedging instruments, they would be able to obtain lower rates. In terms of guarantees, the NCA specifies that they must represent a direct, unconditional petition to the guarantor, and they must be irrevocable instruments expressly related to specific exposures with the coverage clearly defined. In addition, there is a provision for "PD substitution" in which case, if guarantees[57] or credit derivatives[58] are provided, the credit quality of the guarantor (or the seller of protection in the case of derivatives) replaces that of the guaranteed party. What this means is that the portion of exposure supported by such security will be assigned risk weightings attributable to the guarantor that reflect the probability of the guarantor's bankruptcy. The uncovered portion of exposure is given a weighting to reflect the probability of the counterparty's bankruptcy (as determined by the rating).

***

Up until now, we have taken the bank's viewpoint and seen how the relationship between it and its customers is characterized by growing complexity, and at the same time, greater transparency. We have also seen that the bank is the primary entity taking credit risk, which is essentially derived from the characteristics of the counterparty and the transaction and the term of the transaction. When estimating credit risk, we saw that a significant portion of the process is dedicated toward estimating the PD of the borrowing entity.

We will focus specifically on the estimation of the risk of default in the next chapter. Before describing the methods and statistical models used to estimate default risk, it is still necessary to see this from the perspective

---

[57]Unlike the 1988 Accord, the NCA also recognizes guarantees provided by enterprises, and not just those provided by financial institutions.

[58]Only credit default swaps and total return swaps can be considered instruments that can mitigate credit risk in light of the NCA, since they provide protection equivalent to guarantees. We will cover these instruments in greater detail in the next chapter.

of an enterprise. As noted in paragraph four of Chapter 1, default risk is a financial risk of an internal nature that the company may incur for many reasons. These reasons may be tied to both operating and financial activities as well as ineffective treasury management. In any case, default risk occurs upon the permanent inability of the paying entity, to economically meet financial obligations assumed to do business. In these unique ways it differs from liquidity risk, which can also affect a solvent enterprise. In particular, this risk arises when, for operating reasons, there is no longer a match between readily available cash and obligations due on demand, and this was caused by the unstable management of the financial structure which is not consistent with the cash flows generated by the enterprise's operations. A liquidity crisis can result in insolvency only in the case of major treasury management errors or in the case of the embezzlement of liquid assets. In most cases, these two risks are treated as separate risks. In the next chapter, we will see which specific theoretical aspects and practical tools are used to forecast default risk.

The Response to the 2008 Financial Crisis: Basel III and the New Capital Requirements

Basel III: The Genesis

During the 2008 crisis, liquidity became scarce and banks found their self to have insufficient liquidity reserves to meet the obligations and insufficient capital to absorb emerging losses. High leverage amplified losses as banks tried to sell assets into falling and shrinking markets, which created a vicious circle of reducing capital ratios and a need to delever, which increased asset disposals.

Moreover, the procyclicality of Basel II capital formula for credit risk generated an increase in bank's capital requirements, since both the PD and LGD both increased during the crisis. In that situation, several banks had to turn to their central banks for liquidity support and some to their governments for capital injections or support in dealing with assets of uncertain value for which there were no other buyers. In such situation, the G20 asked for a banking reform able to ensure that governments never again have to bail out the banks. They wanted to remove the implicit guarantee that governments will back large banks, if they get into trouble. The G20 did not want to eradicate bank failure nor did it expect central banks to ever have to provide liquidity support to troubled firms.

In response to the crisis, in November 2010, the Basel III proposals for strengthening capital and liquidity standards was ratified by the G20.

The Basel proposals are based on the following objectives:

— Raising the quality, quantity, consistency and transparency of the capital base to ensure that banks are in a better position to absorb losses (Basel II);
— Strengthening the capital requirements for counterparty credit risk (CCR) exposures;
— Introducing a leverage ratio as a supplementary measure to the Basel II risk-based capital;
— Introducing a series of measures to promote the build-up of capital buffers in good times that can be drawn upon in periods of stress;
— Introducing a set of minimum liquidity standard that includes a 30-day liquidity coverage ratio requirement and a longer-term structural liquidity ratio.

In doing so, they committed the global banking industry to significant change and a transition period that extends beyond 2020.

The New Capital Requirements under Basel III

Basel III introduces a new definition of capital to increase the quality, consistency and transparency of the capital base and it also requires higher capital ratios. Key elements of Basel III include:

- Raise quality and quantity of Tier 1 capital.
- Simplification and reduction of Tier 2 capital.
- Elimination of Tier 3 capital.
- More stringent criteria for each instrument.
- Harmonization of regulatory adjustments.
- Introduction of a new limit system for the capital elements.

According to the new definition, capital comprises the following elements:

- Tier 1 capital:
  - Common Equity Tier 1 capital (CET 1 capital).
  - Additional Tier 1 capital.
- Tier 2 capital.

The capital requirements defined by Basel III, as a percentage of RWAs, are the following:

Calibration of the Capital Framework			
Capital requirements and buffers (all numbers in percent)			
	Common Equity (after deductions)	Tier 1 Capital	Total Capital
Minimum	4.5	6.0	8.0
Conservation buffer	2.5		
Minimum plus conservation buffer	7.0	8.5	10.5
Countercyclical buffer range*	0–2.5		

*Common equity or other fully loss absorbing capital.

Under Basel III, total capital ratio will remain 8% of RWAs, while the CET 1 capital ratio increases from 2% to 4.5%. Basel also introduced the additional Tier 1 capital ratio of 1.5%, leading to a Tier 1 capital ratio of 6%. Tier 2 capital decreases by reducing the ratio to 2% of RWA. A key aspect of the stricter definition of capital is that CET 1 instruments[59] — mainly common shares and retained earnings — must be the predominant form of Tier 1 capital.

Additional to these changes, Basel III will introduce two new capital buffers:

— a capital conservation buffer of 2.5%;
— a countercyclical buffer of 0–2.5% depending on macroeconomic circumstances.

For both buffers, an extra cushion of CET 1 capital needs to be held, leading to a CET 1 capital ratio of up to 9.5%.

The Tier 1 capital requirements will be implemented gradually between 2013 and 2015; the capital buffers between 2016 and 2019. The new

---

[59]According to the Basel III proposal, CET 1 items consist of the following instruments: capital instruments, provided the conditions laid down in Article 26 of the proposed EU Regulations are met; share premium accounts, retained earnings, accumulated other comprehensive income, other reserves and funds for general banking risk.

prudential adjustments will be introduced gradually, 20% a year from 2014, reaching 100% in 2018.

Additional Tier 1 capital includes capital instruments (hybrid instruments, contingent capital) that can be converted into CET 1, when CET 1 capital ratio falls below 5.125%. The capital conservation buffer (2.5% of RWA and to be met with CET 1 capital) applies at all times and it is intended to ensure that institutions are able to absorb losses in stress periods lasting for a number of years.

Considering the 4.5% CET 1 capital ratio, institutions must hold 7.0% CET 1 capital on an individual and consolidated basis, at all times.

The level of countercyclical capital buffer is decided by each Member State and it ranges between 0% and 2.5% of RWA and has to be met by CET 1 capital. The aim of this buffer is to increase the financial stability of the system in case of economic downturn by accumulating capital during periods of credit growth.

Liquidity Standards under Basel III

Two liquidity ratios are introduced by Basel III: the Liquidity Coverage Ratio (LCR) and the Net Stable Funding Ratio (NSFR). LCR require banks to hold a buffer of liquid assets to match net liquidity outflows during a 30-day period of stress and it can be written as:

$$LCR = \frac{\text{High quality liquid assets}}{\text{Total net liquidity outflows over 30-day time period}} \geq 100\%.$$

In other terms, banks must have sufficient liquid assets to survive a stress scenario lasting for 30 days. The LCR will be introduced by 2015, after an observation period.

High liquid assets include: cash and deposits held with central banks, transferable assets that are of extremely high liquidity and credit quality, transferable assets representing claims on or guaranteed by the central government of a Member State and transferable assets that are of high liquidity and credit quality.

NSFR requires banks to fund their activities with more stable sources of funding. In particular, banks must maintain a stable funding structure over one year in an extended stress scenario.

$$NSFR = \frac{\text{Available stable funding}}{\text{Required stable funding}} \geq 100\%.$$

The Basel III identifies several levels of "stable funding" that must be considered with different "weights" in the numerator of the formula. Stable funds are considered Tier 1 and 2 capital (weight = 100%), secured and unsecured borrowings with maturity greater than 1 year (100%), preferred stock not included in the Tier 1 with maturity greater than 1 year (weight = 100%), "stable" non-maturity deposits or term deposits with maturity less than 1 year (weight = 90%), "less stable" non-maturity deposits or term deposit with maturity less than 1 year and unsecured wholesale funding (weight = 50%). The required stable funding should be based on the assets liquidity risk of the banks (in-balance and off-balance).

CCR and Banks' Leverage under Basel III

In comparison to Basel II Accord, Basel III strengthens the requirements for the management and capitalization of CCR. It includes an additional capital charge for possible losses associated with deterioration in the creditworthiness of counterparties or increased risk-weights on exposures to large financial institutions (SIFI).

For banks using an IRS to measure credit risk regulatory capital, Basel III requires determining the default risk capital by using the greater of the portfolio-level capital charge based on Effective Expected Positive Exposure (EEPE) using current market data and the one based on EEPE using a stress calibration. Greater EEPEs should not be applied on a counterparty-by-counterparty basis, but on a total portfolio level.

In addition to the default risk capital requirements, Basel III also enhances incentives for clearing over-the-counter (OTC) instruments through central counterparties (CCP). In particular, an additional capital charge to cover the risk of mark-to-market losses on the expected counterparty risk [Credit Valuation Adjustment (CVA)] to OTC derivatives is introduced. The calculation of the CVA charge depends on the method banks use to determine the capital charge for CCR and specific interest rate risk.

To prevent the excessive leverage of financial institutions, Basel III introduces a non-risk based leverage ratio to supplement the risk-based capital framework of Basel II. This new regulatory tool will become a binding instrument only in 2018, after a transition period.

The leverage ratio is calculated by dividing an institution's capital measure by the total exposure. The ratio should be calculated as the simple arithmetic mean of the monthly leverage ratios over a quarter. The numerator of the ratio is the Tier 1 capital, while the denominator is the sum of the exposure values of all assets and off-balance sheet items, not deducted from the calculation of Tier 1 capital.

$$\text{Leverage ratio} = \frac{\text{Tier 1 Capital}}{\text{Total exposure}} \geq 3\%.$$

By 2016, it will be decided, if 3% is an appropriate level for a Tier 1 capital-based leverage ratio and whether the leverage ratio should be the same for all institutions or should differ for various types of institutions. Final adjustments of the ratios would be made in the first half of 2017.

Chapter 4

COMPANY DEFAULT AND DISCRIMINANT VARIABLES FOR SME

Oliviero Roggi and Alessandro Giannozzi

This chapter addresses the relationship between company default and discriminant variables in four industries: Textile, Buildings, Mechanical and Tourism. The dataset is made up of 3,137 Italian small and medium-sized enterprises (SMEs). Results show that the leverage ratios, especially the capitalization level and the interest costs over turnover are good predictors of default, together with the return on sales. Despite that, industry-specific models allow to better identify relevant ratios in each type of business, providing lower classification errors than the general model.

Introduction

Europe's financial landscape is experiencing sweeping changes, driven by a variety of factors, notably the current financial crisis. These changes — in particular the restructuring, consolidation, and reorientation of banking — are likely to affect the financing of small and medium-sized enterprises (SMEs). However, some of these changes may also benefit SME lending under different aspects.

Firstly, new information and communication technologies contribute, at a lower cost, to reducing information asymmetries between lenders and borrowers, thereby making SME lending more attractive. Secondly, partly due to progress in information technology, new banking methods are being developed and implemented. For instance, banks adopt new portfolio credit risk models that allow them to allocate and price their resources more effectively. Thirdly, equity capital is becoming increasingly available to SMEs through the development of secondary capital markets and venture capital finance.

On the other side, several features of Europe's financial landscape have raised concerns about a possible deterioration of conditions for SME finance. Firstly, consolidation in national banking markets has reduced the number of banks and has in many EU countries, especially in the smaller ones, increased the market share of the top-five largest institutions. Moreover, concerns have been raised that the new Basel Capital Accord (Basel II) will change the way banks analyze credits, introducing new credit risk management techniques and possibly reducing the lending activity toward SMEs. This is due to banks' potential perception that SMEs carry higher risk and, hence, higher capital requirements than the ones under Basel I. Many SME associations in different countries have publicly complained about the new rules and many governments are now concerned.

In this scenario, we believe that assessing and pricing SME credit risk correctly is essential for both: financial institutions in order to ensure that the profitability of their commercial clients falls within the desired risk appetite and SMEs in order to guarantee their access to banking funds. Enhancing credit risk models specific for SMEs represents a leading success factor for banks that are interested to target this profitable market.

The main goal of this chapter is to analyze the relationship between company survival and industry-specific discriminant variables in four specific industries: Textile, Buildings, Mechanical and Tourism. In our analysis, we use the definition of SME as stated in new Basel Capital Accord (sales less than 50 million euro) and apply a logit regression analysis to develop the models. We extensively analyze a large number of relevant financial measures in order to select the most predictive ones. Then, we use these variables as predictors of a default event and develop five models: one on each of the four industries and the other on additional businesses (general model). The discriminant variables in the industry-specific models are compared to the variables in the general model in order to identify the specificity of the industry in a surviving company.

The sample for the analysis consisted of 3,137 enterprises: (1,275 defaulted companies and 1,862 non-defaulted companies), spanning the time period 2004–2007.

In section "Default Prediction Methodologies", a survey of the most relevant literature about failure prediction methodologies is provided. First, we give an overview of the most recent studies about SMEs and we analyze their findings. Then, the choice of using a logistic regression to develop a specific SME credit risk model is addressed and justified. The Section "Concept of Default" is dedicated to the choice of the concept of default. In Section "Data Sample", we analyze the dimension and the characteristics of our samples. In Section "Discriminant Variables Definitions and Theoretical Model", we define the financial variables tested in our research, whereas in Section "Treatment of Outliers and Methodology", we explain the process of model building. In Section "Analysis of Results", we develop models to predict default using financial variables for four industry-specific models and for general ones. In Section "Comparing Industry-specific Models to General Model", we provide our conclusions.

Default Prediction Methodologies

The literature about default prediction methodologies is substantial. During the last 40 years, many authors have examined several possible realistic alternatives to predict customers' default or business failure. The seminal works in this field were Beaver (1967) and Altman (1968), who developed univariate and multivariate models to predict business failures using a set of financial ratios. Beaver (1967) used a dichotomous classification test to determine the error rates a potential creditor would experience, if he classified firms on the basis of individual financial ratios as failed or non-failed. He used a matched sample consisting of 158 firms (79 failed and 79 non-failed) and he analyzed 14 financial ratios. Altman (1968) used a multiple discriminant analysis (MDA) technique to solve the ambiguity problem linked to the Beaver's univariate analysis and to assess a more complete financial profile of firms. His analysis drew on a matched sample containing 66 manufacturing firms (33 failed and 33 non-failed) that filed a bankruptcy petition during the period 1946–1965. Altman (1968) examined 22 potentially helpful financial ratios and ended up selecting five, providing in combination, the best overall prediction of corporate bankruptcy.[1] The variables were classified into five standard ratios categories, including liquidity, profitability, leverage, solvency and activity ratios.

For many years thereafter, MDA was the prevalent statistical technique applied to the default prediction models. It was used by many

---

[1] The original Z-score model (Altman, 1968) used five ratios: working capital/total assets, retained earnings/total assets, EBIT/total assets, market value equity/BV of total debt and sales/total assets.

authors (Deakin, 1972; Edmister, 1972; Blum 1974; Altman, Haldeman and Narayanan, 1977; Taffler and Tisshaw 1977; Micha, 1984; Gombola, Haskins, Ketz and Williams 1987; Altman, Hartzell and Peck, 1995; Lussier 1995). However, in most of these studies, authors pointed out that two basic assumptions of MDA are often violated when applied to the default prediction problems.[2] Moreover, in MDA models, the standardized coefficients cannot be interpreted like the slopes of a regression equation and hence do not indicate the relative importance of the different variables. Considering these MDA's problems, Ohlson (1980), for the first time, applied the conditional logit model to the default prediction's study.[3] The practical benefits of the logit methodology are that it does not require the restrictive assumptions of MDA and allows working with disproportional samples.

From a statistical point of view, logit regression seems to fit well the characteristics of the default prediction problem, where the dependant variable is binary (default/non-default) and with the groups being discrete, non-overlapping and identifiable. The logit model yields a score between zero and one which conveniently gives the probability of default of the client.[4] Lastly, the estimated coefficients can be interpreted separately based on the importance or significance of each of the independent variables in the explanation of the estimated probability of default (PD). After the work of Ohlson (1980), most of the academic literature (Zavgren, 1983; Gentry, Newbold and Whitford, 1985; Keasey and Watson, 1991; Aziz, Emanuel and Lawson, 1988; Platt and Platt, 1990; Ooghe, Joos and De Bourdeaudhuij, 1995; Mossman, Bell, Swartz and Turtle, 1998; Charitou and Trigeorgis, 2002; Becchetti and Sierra, 2002) used logit models to predict default. Despite the theoretic differences between MDA and logit analysis, studies (see for example, Lo, 1985) show that empirical results are quite similar in terms of classification accuracy. Indeed, after careful consideration of the nature of the problems and of the purpose of this

---

[2]MDA is based on two restrictive assumptions: (1) the independent variables included in the model are multivariate, normally distributed; (2) the group dispersion matrices (or variance–covariance matrices) are equal across the failing and the non-failing groups. See Barnes (1982); Karels and Prakash (1987); Mc Leay and Omar (2000) for further discussions about this topic.

[3]Zmijewski (1984) was the pioneer in applying probit analysis to predict default, but, until now, logit analysis has given better results in this field.

[4]Critics of the logit technique, including one of the authors of this paper, have pointed out that the specific functional form of a logit regression can lead to bimodal (very low or very high) classification and probabilities of default.

study, we have decided to choose the logistic regression as an appropriate statistical technique.

Concept of Default

Before seeking a default prediction model, it is necessary to clarify the concept of default. From a strictly economic point of view, the concept of default should refer to a client's irreversible financial distress, which will result in failure to respect contractual obligations, rendering probable the loss of a certain quota of the loaned capital.

It is possible, then, to identify various factors that presage failure. The criteria most often used by international banks are the following:

- A bankruptcy (failure) or other legal procedures.
- Debt "restructuring."[5]
- A missing payment after n days (unpaid).
- Depreciation or specific account allowance.
- Problematic debt exposure.

The definition proposed by Basel II foresees exposure leading to default in the independent or concomitant verification of the following credit events[6]:

- Signals indicating a debtor's incapacity to repay a debt (unlikeliness to pay).
- Borrowings for which the bank has made special allowance, depreciation or restructuring plans.
- The other party has presented a bankruptcy suit or other legal procedures.
- Payments are more than 90 days overdue on any bank financial obligation.[7]

The Basel Committee proposed a clear definition of insolvency for internal rating methods. The choice of a single definition is justified by at least two reasons: lack of a clear definition would prevent application of the principle of a "level playing field" across banks and countries, resulting in

---

[5] That is, situations in which a bank, seeing a debtors difficulties, renegotiates contractual conditions.

[6] Basel Committee on Banking Supervision (2003a, 2004a, 2004b).

[7] For Italian credit portfolio, the unpaid limit is increased to 180 days for a transaction period of five years.

substantial differences in the classification of types of default; the second motivation concerns prevention of problems that could emerge in banks' database settings, thus making problematic the process of validation by the banking supervision authorities.

The Basel II definition of default allowed identification of a client's financial distress earlier than had previous definitions, and at the same time avoids problems of excessive subjectivity when classifying corporate exposures. On the other hand, a "delayed" definition of default has the advantage of limiting the subjectivity of the analyst, but would set very low probability of default values, against the loss of great amounts: this would not be a policy for banks.

It is not easy to gather a sample of enterprises using this concept of default. Some of the necessary information is not public, being exclusively available to banks. While the data on failed enterprises is easily found, it is much more difficult to know which enterprises have outstanding debts like those foreseen by the oversight committee. In this study, the data problem has been solved; thanks to the collaboration of several local banks, which have provided the necessary data to develop the models.

Data Sample

The sample for the analysis consisted of 3,137 enterprises: (1,275 defaulted companies and 1,862 non-defaulted companies) (see Table 4.1), spanning the time period 2004–2007. Table 4.2 summarizes the composition of the samples regarding firm's turnover.

Table 4.1:   Dimension of the Sample and Out-of-Sample.

	Textile	Buildings	Mechanical	Tourism	General	Total
Defaulted	180	270	224	117	484	1,275
Non-defaulted	213	378	351	291	629	1,862
Total	393	648	575	408	1,113	3,137

Table 4.2:   Composition of the Samples Regarding Firm's Turnover (Million Euros).

	5–10 (%)	10–25 (%)	25–40 (%)	40–50 (%)	Total (%)
Defaulted	30	45	20	5	100
Non-defaulted	28	53	18	1	100

Companies (in-sample) were selected according to the following criteria from 2004–2007:

- Limited companies (S.r.l. and S.p.A.) localized in Italy.
- Companies not listed on regulated capital markets.
- A turnover above 5 million and below 50 million euros according to SME definition of Basel II Agreement.
- Defaulted companies are selected according to Basel II concept of default: a non-payment after 180 days (unpaid).

Selection criteria were chosen to correctly represent the population of Italian SME. We avoided the introduction of micro-enterprises and market-listed enterprises because their risk factors may be different from the SME ones. Furthermore, this sample is also compliant with the SMEs definition provided by Basel II. Moreover, we excluded banks and other financial companies.

Discriminant Variables Definitions and Theoretical Model

The likelihood that an enterprise will be unable to fulfil its financial obligations can be determined by two factors:

1. Weakening of competitive strength, that is, the contraction of an enterprise's market share relative to competitors, caused, for example, by insufficient technical development or inefficient management of productive processes;
2. Non-sustainability of the debts, due to excessive use of leverage or lack of liquidity "to serve the debt".

The competitive strength of an enterprise can be measured by two aspects. The first is linked to business development; this aspect of management is measured by change rates intervening into elements of balance sheet and income statements such as turnover, fixed assets, net worth, etc. The second relevant aspect is the profitability of the invested capital, and above all the profits derived from core business: obviously, the survival of an enterprise, and the value creation, is linked to obtaining a performance greater than the cost of the capital invested and to economic balance over the long-term.

Signs of weakening in the business development and capital performance indicators can suggest that the core business of the enterprise will not become more remunerative or that the enterprise has not succeeded in

adapting to changes in the market. These aspects, seen in investment policies and in the efficient management of productive processes, can underlie
the financial distress of an enterprise.

The second factor determining insolvency, namely non-sustainability
of a debt, is linked to the financing policies of the enterprise and to it
having a financial structure consistent with the investments made.[8] These
factors are investigated by means of three categories of indicators that
express: the leverage of the enterprise, its capacity — at any point in
time — to confront financial obligations and its exposure to prospective variations in rates of interest. The indicators expressing company
leverage permit investigation of the intensity of the enterprise's leverage
utilization, both for capital employed and for turnover, and also allows
us to assess the consistency between financial structure and investments
made. Obviously, the greater the indebtedness of an enterprise, the greater
the likelihood that it will not fulfil its financial obligations, as negative
economic-cycle or management errors may trigger the onset of difficulty
in repaying loans. Moreover, increased incidence of debt in the financial
structure of an enterprise also exposes it to greater interest rate risk,
because unexpected rate variations will impact heavily on operating costs.
Analysis of liquidity indicators turns to investigation of the enterprise's
capacity to confront short-term debts. It is therefore important to check
whether liquid assets are sufficient to repay short-term debts and also
to verify the capacity of the core business to generate cash flows capable to pay interests. Moreover, analysis of prospective variations in the
commercial policies of the enterprise, in terms of inventories and defer-
ments given to clients and suppliers, is also useful for the evaluation of
liquidity.

These above mentioned relations can be measured with a large number of ratios, which in the literature have been found useful to predict
firms' default.[9] Consistent with the large number of studies discussed
in the section "Default Prediction Methodologies", we use five accounting ratio categories describing the main aspects of a company's financial

---

[8]Investments linked to fixed assets must be financed by means of long-term funding.
The optimal situation, often not practicable, would be to cover fixed assets by means
of own capital. But more usually, fixed investments are financed by recourse debt that
needs to be long-term in order to guarantee consistency between financial structure and
fixed investments.
[9]Chen and Shimerda (1981) show that out of more than 100 financial ratios, almost
50% were found useful in at least one empirical study.

Table **4.3**: Financial Variables.

Category	ID	Variables
Business Development	*B1*	*Turnover variation*
	B2	*Fixed assets variation*
	B3	*(Depreciation fund/fixed assets) variation*
	B4	*Equity variation*
Profitability	*P1*	*EBIT variation*
	P2	*(EBIT + financial profit)/(total assets − non-financial debt)*
	P3	*EBIT/turnover*
	P4	*(EBIT/turnover) variation*
	P5	*Personnel costs/added value*
	P6	*Inventories change/turnover variation*
	P7	*Cost of goods sold/turnover*
	P8	*Added value/fixed asset*
	P9	*EBIT/total investments*
	P10	*Depreciation rate variation*
Interest Rate Risk Exposure	*IR1*	*Interest costs/financial debt*
	IR2	*(EBIT + financial profit)/(total assets − non-financial debt) − (interest costs/financial debt)*
Liquidity	*L1*	*Current ratio*
	L2	*Liquid assets/current assets*
	L3	*Quick ratio*
	L4	*EBITDA/turnover*
	L5	*(Working capital/turnover)*
	L6	*Days of clients variation*
	L7	*Days of inventories variation*
	L8	*Days of debtors variation*
	L9	*(EBITDA − tax)/short term financial debt*
	L10	*(EBITDA − tax)/financial debt*
	L11	*EBITDA/interest costs*
	L12	*Net profit + amortization/short term financial debt*
Leverage	*LE1*	*(Financial debt− cash)/turnover*
	LE2	*(Financial debt− cash)/equity*
	LE3	*(Financial debt− cash)/(equity− intangibile assets)*
	LE4	*Short term financial debt/financial debt*
	LE5	*Equity/fixed assets*
	LE6	*Interest cost/turnover*
	LE7	*Equity/total investments*

profile: liquidity, profitability, leverage, business development and interest rate risk exposure. For each one of these categories, we select a number of financial ratios that were most successful in predicting firms' bankruptcy in the existing studies (see Table 4.3).

In particular, the categories that we define can be described as follows:

- **Business development.** All variables are expressed in terms of variation. Changes in fixed assets, equity, and depreciation funds are investigated as potential sources of company default. Nevertheless, the univariate results have shown that none of those variables are significant in default prediction.
- **Profitability.** In this group, we test 10 variables. According to Altman (1968) and Altman, Haldeman and Narayanan (1977), we investigate the discriminant power of the return on assets (ROA), as well as the relationship between the earnings before interest and taxes (EBIT) and the interest (Altman, Haldeman and Narayanan, 1977). We believe return on sales (ROS) and other similar variables are relevant to predict distress, where the sales margin is particularly low or are not coherent with variables such as the turnover or its variation. The investigation doesn't involve all composition ratios widely used in main literature, such as *Retained Earnings on Total Assets* (Altman, 1968; Altman, Haldeman and Narayanan, 1977), *Net Profit on Total Assets* (Beaver, 1967; Deakin, 1972) and *net profit/equity* or return on equity (ROE). This is mainly because for SME, we believe the net profit can be manipulated by the company's window dressing practices.
- **Interest rate risk exposure.** This group is made of only two variables and is new to this field of research. According to Modigliani and Miller (1958), we believe that PD is lower when *return on debt* (ROD) is low and/or ROD is significantly lower than *return on investment* (ROI).
- Another important aspect of default prediction is the company's **liquidity**. In this group, which is made up of 12 variables, according to Blum (1974), Beaver (1967), Deakin (1972), we investigate the discriminant power of cash flow [earnings before interest, taxes, depreciation, and amortization (EBITDA)] on financial debt ratio and the relationship between cash flow and current liabilities (Edmister, 1972). In addition, we test the "traditional" variables such as the current ratio (Beaver, 1967; Altman, Haldeman and Narayanan, 1977) and the quick ratio.

According to main Italian default risk studies (Alberici, 1975; Luerti, 1987), we also test the prediction power of the days of inventories' variation, days of debtors, and days of client variations. Nevertheless, the univariate results have shown that none of these variations are significant in default prediction.

- **Leverage.** This group is made of seven variables. We tested the composition index such as the equity on total assets ratio (Deakin, 1972) and the equity on fixed assets ratio (Alberici, 1975). In addition, we used the net financial position on turnover ratio and included in this group of variables another index, such as the interest costs on turnover.

Treatment of Outliers and Methodology

During the analysis, we analyzed and treated all outliers that could determine significant distortions in the development of the models. We defined all outliers as values 2.5 standard deviations away from the mean and we replaced them according to winsorization methods. The "boundary values" are calculated as follows:

Population Mean $\pm$ (2.5 $*$ Standard Deviation).

This allowed us to improve the performance of the models while maintaining the original size of the sample. During the analysis, we took the natural logarithm of some of the variables. First, we tested the prediction power of each variable, both in its original and logarithmic form, using the following equation:

$$\ln\frac{a}{b} = \ln a - \ln b. \tag{1}$$

When the variable showed a negative value, we applied the Equation (2) where the possible negative value is "drawn out" from the application of the logarithm to the absolute value of the numerator and the denominator:

$$F1: a/b = \text{Sign of } a * [\ln(|a+1|)] - \text{Sign of } b * [\ln(|b+1|)]. \tag{2}$$

We defined this transformation as "$F1$". This transformation provides a double advantage. On the one hand, it obtains in any way the "beneficial effects" of the logarithm in terms of statistic distribution of data and on the other hand, it keeps the sign of the ratio. This transformation improved significantly the results of the model.

Ultimately, we develop the model using an iterative process, similar to a logit stepwise methodology. In this way, we ensure that the model with the highest discriminatory power is chosen. In addition to the correlation analysis, we checked that the sign of the coefficient was consistent with the theoretical ratio between the insolvency risk and the variable itself and the mono-tonicity of the variable.

Table 4.4:   The Textile Model.

Weight	Variables	Intensity in Term of Variability Explained	Category
−0.67113* −0.26620**	Equity/total investments	+ + ++	Leverage
−0.08669	EBIT/turnover	+ + ++	Profitability
1.73975	Interest costs/turnover	++	Leverage

Notes: *For positive value of the ratio; **For negative value of the ratio.

Analysis of Results

The Model for the Textile Industry

After running the logistic regression, we find three financial variables to do the best overall job together in predicting default (see Table 4.4). We find that enterprise capitalization level (equity/total investments) and the ROS (EBIT/turnover) have the highest discriminatory power for fashion/textile Italian SME.

This empirical evidence is not a surprise because the ROS explains the core business profitability, which has a very high signalling value in predicting financial distress. In fact, a low ROS is a signal that the company may have financial problems in the future.

Regarding the equity over total investment, we note a non-linear correlation with default risk. To improve the aggregate performance of our model, we test the discriminant power, both for positive and negative values of equity. Differences in weights (from −0.67113 for positive values to −0.26620 for negative values) allow us to think that when equity > 0, this ratio is more important than for negative values.

In addition, interest costs over turnover seem to be good predictors of default. This variable is an extension of the enterprise capitalization level because it depends on the level of the financial debt, which identifies the impact of debt on company profitability.

These results led us to conclude that in the fashion/textile industry, the insolvency risk depends on the indicators of leverage (equity/total assets and interest cost/turnover) and the ROS. The achievement of high ROS and high capitalization level could be relevant for a company's survival.

Regarding the accuracy of the textile model, results show that 159 enterprises are correctly classified as non-defaulted, corresponding to 75.35% of the non-defaulted sample and 111 enterprises are classified as defaulted (80.43% of the total default sample). This implies that

Table 4.5: In-Sample Classification Results of the Fashion/Textile Model.

		Y Classified		Total Data Used
Y True		0	1	
	0	159	52	211
		75.35%	24.64%	
	1	27	111	138
		19.56%	80.43%	
Area under receiver operating characteristics				
(ROC) curve = 82.20%				349
Mean Error = 22.63%				

Table 4.6: The Buildings Model.

Weight	Variables	Intensity in Term of Variability Explained	Category
−0.62571*	Equity/total investments	+ + + +	Leverage
−0.31306**			
−0.089	EBIT/turnover	+ + + +	Profitability
0.36234	Interest costs/financial debt	+ +	Leverage
0.62639	Interest costs/turnover	+	Leverage

Notes: *For positive value of the ratio; **For negative value of the ratio.

the remaining enterprises were incorrectly classified with a Type 1 error (defaulted enterprises classified as non-defaulted) of 19.56% and a Type 2 error (non-defaulted enterprises classified as defaulted) of 24.64% (see Table 4.5).

The Model for the Buildings Industry

We find that enterprise capitalization level (equity/total investments) and the ROS (EBIT/turnover) have the highest discriminatory power for buildings companies. In addition, interest cost over financial debt (ROD) and interest expenses/turnover seem to be good predictors of default (see Table 4.6).

These results led us to conclude that in the Buildings industry, the insolvency risk depends on the indicators of leverage (equity/total assets, cost of financing and interest cost/turnover) and with a lower prediction power on the ROS.

Regarding the accuracy of the Buildings model, results show that 267 enterprises are correctly classified as non-defaulted, corresponding to 78.53% of the non-defaulted sample and 111 enterprises are classified

Table 4.7: In-Sample Classification Results of the Buildings Model.

		Y Classified		Total Data Used
Y True		0	1	
	0	267	73	340
		78.53%	21.47%	
	1	42	111	153
		27.45%	72.55%	
Area under ROC curve = 81.2%				493
Mean error = 23.3%				

Table 4.8: The Mechanical Model.

Weight	Variables	Intensity in Term of Variability Explained	Category
1.64372	Interest costs/turnover	+ + + +	Leverage
−0.35047*	Equity/total investments		
−0.15131**		+ + + +	Leverage
−0.07921	EBIT/turnover	+ +	Profitability
−0.06704	Working capital/turnover	+	Liquidity

Notes: *For positive value of the ratio; **For negative value of the ratio.

as defaulted (72.55% of the total default sample). This implies that the remaining enterprises were incorrectly classified with a Type 1 error (defaulted enterprises classified as non-defaulted) of 27.45% and a Type 2 error (non-defaulted enterprises classified as defaulted) of 21.47% (see Table 4.7).

The Model for the Mechanical Industry

We find that interest costs over turnover has the highest prediction power in the mechanical industry. In addition, similar to other industries, the enterprise capitalization level and the ROS are still good predictors of default. Differently from other businesses, one liquidity ratio seems to have a relevant prediction power (see Table 4.8).

These results led us to conclude that in the mechanical industry, the insolvency risk depends on the indicators of leverage (interest costs/turnover, equity/total assets), on the ROS and on the liquidity position of the firm (working capital/turnover).

Regarding the accuracy of the Mechanical model, results show that 237 enterprises are correctly classified as non-defaulted, corresponding

Table 4.9:   In-Sample Classification Results of the Mechanical Model.

	Y Classified		Data Utilization
Y True	0	1	
0	237	80	317
	74.76%	25.24%	
1	37	125	162
	22.84%	77.16%	
Area under ROC curve = 80.8%			479
Mean error = 24.4%			

Table 4.10:   The Tourism Model.

Weight	Variables	Intensity in Term of Variability Explained	Category
−3.7828	Equity/financial debt	+ + ++	Leverage
0.6432	Interest costs/turnover	+ + +	Leverage
−0.07921	Cost of goods sold/turnover	++	Profitability
−0.06704	Total assets	+	Size

to 74.76% of the non-defaulted sample and 125 enterprises are classified as defaulted (77.16% of the total default sample). This implies that the remaining enterprises were incorrectly classified with a Type 1 error (defaulted enterprises classified as non-defaulted) of 22.84% and a Type 2 error (non-defaulted enterprises classified as defaulted) of 25.24% (see Table 4.9).

The Model for the Tourism Industry

We find that equity over financial debt has the highest prediction power in the mechanical industry. In addition, similar to other industries, interest costs over turnover is a good predictor of default. Differently from other businesses, the company size and the costs efficiency (cost of goods sold/turnover) are relevant predictors of default (see Table 4.10).

These results led us to conclude that in the tourism industry, the insolvency risk depends on the indicators of leverage (interest costs/turnover, equity/financial debts), on the costs efficiency and on the company size (total assets).

Regarding the accuracy of the Tourism model, results show that 163 enterprises are correctly classified as non-defaulted, corresponding to 72.77% of the non-defaulted sample and 65 enterprises are classified

Table 4.11: In-Sample Classification Results of the
Tourism Model.

		Y Classified		Data Utilization
Y True		0	1	
	0	163	61	224
		72.77%	27.23%	
	1	14	65	79
		17.72%	82.28%	
Area under ROC curve = 80.1%				303
Mean error = 25.75%				

Table 4.12: The General Model.

Weight	Variables	Intensity in Term of Variability Explained	Category
−0.31982	Equity/total investments	+ + ++	Leverage
−0.16335	Quick ratio	+ + +	Liquidity
0.27952	Interest costs/turnover	+ + +	Leverage
0.15362	Interest costs/financial debts	+ +	Interest rate risk
−0.03332	EBIT/turnover	+	Profitability

as defaulted (82.28% of the total default sample). This implies that
the remaining enterprises were incorrectly classified with a Type 1 error
(defaulted enterprises classified as non-defaulted) of 17.72% and a Type 2
error (non-default enterprises classified as defaulted) of 27.23% (see
Table 4.11).

The General Model

After running the logistic regression, we find five financial variables to do
the best overall job together in predicting default (see Table 4.12). We
find that enterprise capitalization level (*equity/total investments*) has the
highest discriminatory power for Italian SME. This can be explained by
the fact that Italian SMEs present a lower capitalization level compared
to their European counterparts. The higher financial debt allows the percentage of equity on total investments to better discriminate enterprises in
default. Moreover, the *quick ratio* and *the incidence of financial charge over
turnover*, show a higher discriminant power but a lower power in respect
to previous indicators. In fact, the presence of liquid asset to cover current
liabilities, covers financial obligations on time. Moreover, interest cost over

turnover depends on the level of financial debt, which identifies the impact of debt on company profitability.

In addition, *interest cost over financial debt* and *EBIT/turnover* have a more limited discriminant power. In particular, the ROS seems not that important, in predicting default risk, when a general approach is applied. Concerning other group of variables tested, not all the "business development" regressors were found statistically significant. Only turnover variable was slightly correlated with default risk. This result did not surprise us due to the nature of the variation of the above mentioned indicators.[10]

Table 4.12 shows the discriminant variables for the general model and the intensity of the relationship with the default risk measured in terms of variability explained.

Regarding the accuracy of the general model, results show that 699 enterprises are correctly classified as non-defaulted, corresponding to 75.73% of the total non-defaulted sample and 244 enterprises are correctly classified as defaulted (80.43% of the defaulted sample). This implies that the remaining enterprises are incorrectly classified with a Type 1 error (defaulted enterprises classified as non-defaulted) of 29.27% and a Type 2 error of 24.27%. In addition, we measured the area under ROC curve as 72.80% (see Table 4.13).

Comparing Industry-Specific Models to General Model: Conclusions

Ultimately, we compare the results of the industry-specific models and the general model in terms of discriminant variables. Table 4.14 summarizes

Table 4.13: In-Sample Classification Results of the General Model.

		Y Classified		Total Data Used
		0	1	
Y True				
	0	699	224	923
		75.73%	24.27%	
	1	101	244	345
		29.27%	80.43%	
Area under ROC curve = 72.80%				1268
Mean error = 25.63%				

[10]Often these variables present several negative and positive values in each of the two groups of enterprises (*non-default* and *default*), that invalidate the discriminant power of the type of indicators for the model assessment.

Table 4.14:   Comparison between Industry-Specific Models and General Model.

Variables	Category	Textile	Buildings	Mechanical	Tourism	General
Equity/total assets	Leverage	X	X	X	—	X
Interest costs/ turnover	Leverage	X	X	X	X	X
EBIT/turnover	Profitability	X	X	X	—	X
Interest costs/ financial debt	Interest rate risk	—	X	—	—	X
Working capital/ turnover	Liquidity	—	—	X	—	—
Equity/financial debt	Leverage	—	—	—	X	—
Cost of goods sold/turnover	Profitability	—	—	—	X	—
Total assets	Size	—	—	—	X	—
Quick ratio	Liquidity	—	—	—	—	X

the results of the models and allow us to identify the specificity of each industry.

The capitalization level and the interest costs over turnover are important in a company surviving independently from the type of business. The ROS has a good prediction power in four of the five models, while the liquidity ratios and the business development ratio are not relevant in the default risk estimation. Nevertheless, the "weights" of the ratios change in each type of business and better classification results can be obtained using industry-specific models.

Chapter 5

DEFAULT RISK AND DISCRIMINANT METHODOLOGIES FOR SME

Oliviero Roggi and Alessandro Giannozzi

This chapter aims at a better understanding of the effectiveness and efficiency of methodologies that estimate default risk, for both general and industry specific models. The main research question is "how is the probability of default efficiently estimated according to Basel II?" This implies testing for the best methodology to discriminate between *"in bonis"* and "in default" companies within the Basel II concept of "default". Results based on a parity sample of 300 + 300 Italian companies show that Multivariate Discriminant Analysis (MDA) or Discriminant Analysis by Generalized Estimating Equations approach (DA-GEE) and Logit Regression (LR) provide better estimation of Default Risk than can Partial Least Squared Regression Discriminant Analysis (PLS-DA). Using PLS-DA, 42% of these companies fall into the overlapping area (grey zone); using DA-GEE and LR, respectively, only 31% and 29% of companies are misclassified. Industry-specific models offer a more efficient classification of the default when compared to the general model, but percentage of errors are not significantly lower.

An Empirical Research on SMEs Default: Research Questions and Methodology

As mentioned in Chapter 3, Basel Committee on Banking Supervision introduced a series of innovations that impact significantly on the business of credit risk management by banks, with consequences for strategies of capital lending to enterprises.[1] Basel II has modified the method for

---

[1]The bank loans are, for small and medium-sized enterprise (SME), the most important source of funds to finance business development and investments.

calculating the capital requirements that banks should respect in order to sustain the credit risk entailed in a lending portfolio. Basel II foresees the implementation of rating systems to evaluate the credit standing of corporate clients.

The accuracy of models to predict insolvency is of interest to researchers — and indeed to all others "obliged" to take "internal rating models" into consideration (banks and enterprises). In particular, for enterprises, self-evaluation of credit standing enables the entrepreneur to understand which variables will be most significant for deciding its banking rating, so that optimization of financial structures becomes both possible and desirable.

This research therefore proposes to verify and compare the predictive efficacy of the most commonly employed statistical methodologies used to predict corporate insolvency, using a parity sample of selected enterprises and employing the Basel II concept of default. The definition given by the Basel Committee, namely the proxy of a default, identifies a credit event in the life of an enterprise, taking place before the legal declaration of failure (bankruptcy), namely a situation of insolvency regarding any financial obligation to a bank that is overdue by at least 90 days. The statistical methodologies to be compared are as follows: Multivariate Discriminant Analysis (MDA) or Discriminant Analysis by Generalized Estimating Equations approach (DA-GEE), Logistic Regression (LR), and Discriminant-Partial Least Squared Regression Analysis (DA-PLS). Although not yet much used to estimate default, this last methodology offers useful elements for methodological reflection by the research community. Evaluating the applicability of PLS regression to the research problem and to the question of the efficacy of prediction models for insolvency "dynamics" allows us to consider the dynamic of deterioration in the financial situation of an enterprise (financial variables of three consecutive years). This enables methodological comparison of classification results, so as to identify the best analytical instrument to apply.

This study looks at the default risk of SMEs operating in the Italy. The geographical limitation reduces the statistical population of the analysis, but enables identification of possible sources of risk due to the location of the enterprise in a particular economic, political and local setting. Rating agencies indeed frequently consider geographical location a relevant variable in the determination of default risk.[2]

---

[2]For example, Standard & Poor's (2002) modified the credit rating according to geographical location and to the different interest rates contracted all over Italy.

A final objective of this chapter is to compare the predictive accuracy of "general" and "industry-specific" models[3] so that each model reflects the credit risk factors relevant to that particular industry.

Summarising, the main research question is: *"how can the probability of default be efficiently estimated according to Basel II?"* This implies testing for the best methodology to discriminate between "in bonis" and "in default" companies. The final proposition to be tested concerns model generalization: *"Industry specific models are more efficient in estimating default risk than is a general model"*.

The Interpretative Model: Discriminant Variables

Thirty five financial variables were selected with reference to the core academic literature. A detailed description of variables is provided in the section "Discriminant Variables Definitions and Theoretical Model" of Chapter 4. Extensive balance-sheet indicators were grouped in five categories. Table 5.1 summarizes the univariate prediction power of each variable.

Data Sample

The initial sample for analysis was composed of 300 + 300 enterprises selected according to the following criteria for the period 1999–2004:

— Limited companies localised in Tuscany;
— Not listed on regulated capital markets;
— Revenues over 5 million and below 50 million euro;
— Business sectors–Atecofin codes.

    ○ Textiles and fashion,
    ○ Mechanical industries,
    ○ Buildings industry.

These selection criteria were identified to correctly represent the population of enterprises in the Italian economy, avoiding possible distortions due to the introduction of micro-enterprises and market listed enterprises,[4]

---

[3]Industry identification is based on Atecofin codes: www.agenziaentrate.it.

[4]Data published by rating agencies shows that the size of an enterprise is also a variable that impacts on default risk, in so far as the default rates are much higher for micro-enterprises, and decrease with increases in scales of business.

Table 5.1: Univariate Prediction Power of Each Variable.

Variables	Category	t-ratio	Prob $> |t|$
Turnover variation	Business Development	0.778732	0.4369
Fixed assets variation		1.335255	0.1839
(Depreciation fund/fixed assets) variation		—	—
Number of employees variation		−0.5392	0.5904
Equity variation		3.683537	0.0003
EBIT variation	Profitability	2.435541	0.0161
(EBIT + financial profit)/(total assets − non-financial debt)		2.238769	0.0265
EBIT/fatturato		3.094756	0.0024
(EBIT/turnover) variation		2.647655	0.0092
Personnel costs/added variation		0.396888	0.6921
Inventories change/turnover variation		−0.34453	0.7309
Cost of goods sold/turnover		−2.64019	0.0093
Added value/fixed assets		—	—
Added value/number of employees		1.217004	0.2259
Depreciation rate variation		—	—
Interest costs/financial debt	Rate Risk	−0.91077	0.3651
(EBIT + financial profit)/(total assets − non-financial debt) − (interest costs/financial debt)		1.757941	0.0825
Current ratio	Liquidity	0.383757	0.7016
Liquid assets/current assets		2.822134	0.0054
Quick ratio		1.717038	0.0883
EBITDA/turnover		2.768848	0.0065
(Working capital/turnover)		0.832928	0.4065
Days of clients variation		−0.88238	0.3801
Days of inventories variation		−1.72967	0.0853
Days of debtors variation		−0.68972	0.4916
(EBITDA − tax)/short term financial debt		2.047004	0.0440
(EBITDA − tax)/financial debt		1.885294	0.0631
EBITDA/interest costs		2.934433	0.0039
Net profit + amortization/short term financial debt		2.093261	0.0395
(Financial debt − cash)/turnover	Leverage	−4.58462	<0.0001
(Financial debt − cash)/equity		−2.04809	0.0423
(Financial debt − cash)/(equity − intangibile assets		−1.08418	0.2793
Short term financial debt/financial debt		1.086872	0.2788
Equity/fixed assets		−1.00342	0.3176
Intangibile costs/total assets		−1.84624	0.0663

for which the risk factors may be very different from those of SMEs. This sample also conforms to the definition of SMEs given by Basel II.

Data was collected for each enterprise for three years of balance-sheets, following the sampling schema below and the summary report provided by the "Centrale dei Rischi", which lists variables illustrating the relation between the enterprise and the banking system.

Entering into the detail of the sampling process, two different designs have been used: following a first, more traditional, design, the balance-sheets of N_D enterprises in default were chosen all in the same year, for example 2000. Between the N_D enterprises in the sample, N_1, failed in 2001, others, N_2 after two years in 2002 and finally the last, N_3, after three years, in 2003. Obviously, $N_1 + N_2 + N_3 = N_D$. Analogously, the balance-sheets of the N_B in bonis enterprises all refer to the same year, 2000. In this approach, each enterprise is represented by just one balance-sheet, as given in Table 5.2.

Following a second data sampling, the balance-sheets of N_D businesses in default, for example in 2003, are examined for the three *consecutive* years preceding their default: 2000, 2001 and 2002, as given in Table 5.3.

$N_{D,3}$ gives the total of the N_D balance-sheets for businesses failed in the first observation year, namely *three years before* the default, and thus

Table 5.2: First Design for Sample of Businesses in Bonis e in Default: Traditional Statistical Techniques.

1999	2000	2001	2002	2003	2004
—	N_1	D	—	—	—
—	N_2	—	D	—	—
—	N_3	—	—	D	—
—	—	—	—	—	—
—	N_B	—	—	—	—

Table 5.3: Second Design for Sample of Businesses in Bonis e in Default: Innovative DA-PLS Technique.

1999	2000	2001	2002	2003	2004
—	—	D	—	—	—
—	—	—	D	—	—
—	$N_{D,3}$	$N_{D,2}$	$N_{D,1}$	D	—
—	—	—	—	—	D
—	—	—	—	—	—
—	$N_{B,3}$	$N_{B,2}$	$N_{B,1}$	—	—

also for the following two years. In the same way, the balance-sheets of N_B in bonis businesses are examined for the same three years: 2000, 2001 and 2002. According to this approach, each enterprise is represented in the database by three balance-sheets for three consecutive years.

Methods of Analysis

This study applies statistical methodologies to the sample design described above. Following the first sampling design, the economic and financial indicators are not auto-correlated.[5] This allows us to use "classical" methods, namely DA, LR, to treat the data.

Using the second sampling design, a high degree of auto-correlation is almost certain between indicators. It makes it suitable to use different testing methods that have recently become available: PLS-DA, the method used in this study; cluster analysis on PLS components with attribution to the nearest group; PLS logistic regression[6] (Logit-PLS); and PLS typological regression[7] (PLS-TR).

PLS regression, recently perfected by Tenenhaus (1995), is based on the non-linear iterative partial least squares (NIPALS) algorithm. It relates two matrices of variables, the independent X and the dependent Y. From matrix X the algorithm extracts PLS components which, at the same time, summarise the variable X and explain the dependent variables Y.

Compared to other methods, the principal advantages of the PLS regressions are:

— PLS solves the problem of missing data: the algorithm can be run with missing values.
— Observations matrix J_X of independent variables and matrix J_Y made by dependent variables can be correlated.
— Some, or even all, of the J_X independent variables and the J_Y dependent variables can be qualitative or nominal in type.

This research paper uses PLS regression, running the statistical software Simca P, which utilizes a NIPALS algorithm. Table 5.4 gives an example of PLS output achieved by Simca P.

---

[5] We refer to correlation between variables at time t and $t-1$.
[6] Vinzi and Tenenhaus (2000). The classic logistic regression could be applied to PLS significant components.
[7] Vinzi and Lauro (2002).

Table 5.4: Example of Output Provided by Simca P.

Comp. PLS =	R2X	R2X (cum.)	Eigen value	R2Y	R2Y (cum.)	Q2	Limit	Q2 (cum.)	Sign.	Num. Iterazi
1	—	—	—	—	—	—	—	—	—	—
2	—	—	—	—	—	—	—	—	—	—

where

$$R2X = \sum_{j=1}^{J} R^2(\pmb{x}_j, \pmb{t}_a) / J_X = \sum_{j=1}^{J} corr^2(\pmb{x}_j, \pmb{t}_a) / J_X$$

$$= \text{Fraction of Sum of Squares (SS) of all the } X's$$
$$\text{explained by the } a^{\text{ma}} \text{ component PLS } t_a. \quad (1)$$

$$R2X(\text{cum.}) = \sum_{a=1}^{A} R^2 X = \sum_{a=1}^{A} corr^2(\pmb{x}_j, \pmb{t}_a) / J_X$$

$$= \text{Cumulative SS of all the } X's \text{ explained by all}$$
$$\text{extracted components.} \quad (2)$$

Eigenvalue = Eigenvalue of the X matrix.

$$R2Y = R^2(\pmb{y}, \pmb{t}_a) = corr^2(\pmb{y}, \pmb{t}_a)$$
$$= \text{Fraction of SS of all the } Y's \text{ explained by } a^{\text{ma}} \quad (3)$$
$$\text{component PLS } t_a.$$

$$R2Y(\text{cum.}) = \sum_{a=1}^{A} R^2 Y = \sum_{a=1}^{A} corr^2(\pmb{y}, \pmb{t}_a)$$
$$= \text{The cumulative SS of all the } Y's \text{ explained by the}$$
$$\text{extracted components.} \quad (4)$$
$$Q2 = Q^2 = \text{The fraction of the total variation of the}$$
$$X's \text{ (PC) and } Y's \text{ (PLS) that can be predicted by the}$$
$$\text{current component.}$$

Simca estimate for each PLS components has two values: $\hat{y}_{ai}$ predicted with all I observation e $\hat{y}_{a(-i)}$ obtained excluding the observation i. For each observation it estimates the residual, obtaining $RSS_a = Residual\ Sum\ of$

Squares e $\text{PRESS}_a = Predicted\ Error\ Sum\ of\ Squares$ di $\boldsymbol{y}$,

$$\text{RSS}_a = \sum_{i=1}^{I}(y_i - \hat{y}_{ai})^2 \quad e \quad \text{PRESS}_a = \sum_{i=1}^{I}(y_i - \hat{y}_{a(-i)})^2. \quad (5)$$

Simca estimate for each PLS components:

$$Q_a^2 = 1 - \frac{\text{PRESS}_a}{\text{RSS}_{a-1}}. \quad (6)$$

Limit = The cross validation threshold for that component. When $Q2 >$ Limit, the component is significant. The limit is 0.0975.

$$\boldsymbol{Q2}(\textbf{cum.}) = \sum_{k=1}^{a} Q_k^2 = \text{The cumulative } Q2 \text{ for all the } X's \text{ (PC) and}$$

$$Y'S \text{ (PLS) for the extracted components.} \quad (7)$$

Sign. = Significance of the component according to cross validation rules: $R1$, $R2$, NS, $N3$, $N4$, NE.

The first PLS component t_a is extracted in the following process:

$$\boldsymbol{t}_1 = w_{11}\boldsymbol{x}_1 + w_{12}\boldsymbol{x}_2 + \cdots + w_{1j}\boldsymbol{x}_j + \cdots + w_{1J}\boldsymbol{x}_J, \quad (8)$$

where

$$w_{1j} = \frac{corr(\boldsymbol{x}_j, \boldsymbol{y})}{\sqrt{\sum_{j=1}^{J} corr^2(\boldsymbol{x}_j, \boldsymbol{y})}}. \quad (9)$$

After this, the software calculates a simple regression

$$\boldsymbol{y} = c_1 \boldsymbol{t}_1 + \boldsymbol{y}_1, \quad (10)$$

where c_1 is the slope coefficient and $\boldsymbol{y}_1$ the vector residual. Joining the two equations gives:

$$\boldsymbol{y} = c_1 w_{11}\boldsymbol{x}_1 + c_1 w_{12}\boldsymbol{x}_2 + \cdots + c_1 w_{1j}\boldsymbol{x}_j + \cdots + c_1 w_{1J}\boldsymbol{x}_{1J} + \boldsymbol{y}_1. \quad (11)$$

The second PLS component is estimated by the residual vector of first one.

Exploratory Analysis and Treatment of Outliers

This study used and tested a very extensive group of indicators, which then required an exploratory analysis[8] of the variables, aiming at:

— Identification of outlier values;
— Identification of univariate predictive power of variables (ANOVA);
— Analysis of correlation matrices and selection of independent variables by means of an iterative process.[9]

During the analysis, we found and treated all outlier values, which could cause heavy distortions in the development of the models. In most cases we found outlier data was not relevant in describing the current financial situation of the enterprise.

In developing the model, we defined outliers as those (superior or inferior) values for each variable that are two standard deviations away from the mean of the values in the population and we replace these according to winsorization methods. The "boundary values", are calculated as follows:

$$\textbf{Population mean} \pm (\textbf{2} * \textbf{Standard Deviation}).$$

This enabled us to improve the performance of the models while maintaining the original characteristics of the data.

Analysis of Results

Traditional Techniques and Prediction of Default Risk

Regarding the traditional techniques, a general model and three sectoral models were developed for both DA-GEE and LR, therefore totalling eight statistical models besides those carried out using DA-PLS. The results were as follows.

Results of general models

The general models were assessed on the basis of a sample of $124 + 126$ enterprises, of which 248 were classified. Two observations were excluded as outliers for both methodologies. DA-GEE correctly classified 106 in bonis

---

[8]For the exploratory analysis we used the JMP 6.0 SAS Institute software.
[9]We used a stepwise regression to identify the multivariate predictive power of variables.

enterprises, namely 80.3% of the total and 66 in default enterprises, namely 56.9% of the total. The logistic regression, in contrast, correctly assessed the status of 104 in bonis enterprises and 71 in default, namely respective to 78.79% and 61.21% of each of the two classes. This means that the remaining enterprises are erroneously classified with Type 1 percentage errors (in default enterprises classified in bonis by the model) as high. This could be due to the non-homogeneity of the data, in so far as the enterprises analyzed have very different structures of balance-sheet indicators according to the business they pursue; or could be due to the default event used. In fact, enterprises considered in default are those with 180 days "outstanding debt" — even if in some cases the situation might yet be recuperated. Thus the modelling of this data is more complex because the difference between the balance-sheet indicators of the two groups of enterprises is lower than in the legal failures based model (see Tables 5.5 and 5.6).

Results of the industry-specific models

As regards the six models for textiles, the construction and mechanical industries, all the methodologies give the following results.

Contrary to what has been seen analytically in the general model, we present the sectoral classification results in summary. Only one percentage

Table **5.5**:   Classification Results: DA-GEE.

Count Col %	Actual 0	Actual 1	Total Sample
Pred 0	106	50	—
	80.30%	43.10%	
Pred 1	26	66	—
	19.70%	56.90%	
Size	132	116	248

Table **5.6**:   Classification Results: LR.

Count Col %	Actual 0	Actual 1	Total Sample
Pred 0	104	45	—
	78.79%	38.79%	
Pred 1	28	71	—
	21.21%	61.21%	
Size	132	116	248

Table 5.7: LR *vs.* DA-GEE.

	General Model		Textile Model		Buildings Model		Mechanical Industry Model	
	%	%	%	%	%	%	%	%
Methodology	*Correct*	*Error*	*Correct*	*Error*	*Correct*	*Error*	*Correct*	*Error*
DA-GEE	69	31	80.6	19.4	99	1	72	28
LR	71	29	81	19	99	1	73	27

indicator of error in the model is shown, calculated as the weighted average of Type 1 and 2 errors.

By definition more homogenous, this data gives a more correct classification percentage than does the general model, except in the mechanical industry case. This could be due to the heterogeneous business activities in this sector. The lowest percentage of error (1%) is seen in the construction industry model, where the balance-sheet structures record strong similarities across the enterprises, although this could also reflect the limited scale of the sample (see Table 5.7).

All this demonstrates that the estimation of models based on enterprises with homogeneous activities and data are much more satisfactory and permit adoption of a final proposition, affirming that *industry specific models, limited to traditional techniques, predict defaults with greater efficacy than do general models.*

Results of the PLS Regression

PLS-DA was applied to a general model and to three industry-specific models. The PLS regression used a data panel (for the balance-sheets of three years prior to the default) collected according to the second sample design described above and accounting for temporal dynamics of deterioration in the financial situation of the enterprise.

Regarding the quality and accuracy[10] of the model, we confirm that:

— Using the cross validation method, only a principal component gives a significant result ($R1$);

---

[10]Our empirical study on the applicability of the PLS regression is certainly not exhaustive. Moreover, for the estimating of a "dynamic" model we could apply a cluster analysis on PLS significant compenents or a typological regression. However, we chose not to use these methods because PLS does not give useful model results.

Table 5.8:   PLS Regression: Results.

	PLS Significant Components	R2X	R2Y	% Error	Y-Predicted Overlapping Area	% of Companies In the Overlapping Area
General Model	1	0.22	0.13	29.80	0.25<Y>0.70	73
Textile Model	1	0.285	0.299	20.60	0.30<Y>0.60	48
Buildings Model	1	0.352	0.532	16.70	0.30<Y>0.40	22
Mechanical Model	1	0.289	0.222	22.70	0.35<Y>0.60	60

— There is low capacity $(R2X)$ to summarize the information of the matrix of regressors, because at maximum 35.2% (construction model) of the variance of the original matrix is explained by the principal components;

— There is low capacity $(R2Y)$ to identify the principal components adequately correlated to the predicted values Y; in fact only the construction sector model achieves a satisfactory level (53.20%);

— There is an extensive range of overlap in the values of the predicted values of model Y, as seen in the Table 5.8;

— A high percentage of observations are noted in the overlapping area.[11]

One notable aspect is the considerable improvement in the PLS regression results for the industry specific model. In fact, remaining at contained levels, the capacity of the PLS components to "explain" default status improves at the same time that it reduces the range of overlap of the Y-predicted values and the number of enterprises in the gap.

PLS, moreover, provides percentages of correct classification similar to traditional methodologies, but it shows a strong aggregation of the Y-predicted results by the model — this last factor suggests that running "dynamic" models based on three balance-sheet years is not practicable, or at any rate not useful.

As previously explained, this allows us to confirm that PLS is not a methodology suited to the estimation of default risk, at least within the confines of this research. Although ineffective at predicting default, nonetheless the PLS industry-specific analysis gives a better quality of model than the general one — confirming our last proposition.

---

[11]This area is the graphics zone where Y-predicted values overlap.

Table 5.9:   Summary of Classification Results: DA-GEE *vs.* LR *vs.* PLS-DA.

Methodology	General Model		Textile Model		Construction Industry Model		Manufacturing Model	
	% Correct	*% Error*	*% Correct*	*% Error*	*% Correct*	*% Error*	*% Correct*	*% Error*
DA-GEE	69	*31*	*80.6*	*19.4*	*99*	*1*	*72*	*28*
LR	*71*	*29*	*81*	*19*	—	—	*73*	*27*
PLS-DA	*70.20*	*29.80*	*79.40*	*20.60*	*83.30*	*16.70*	*77.30*	*22.70*

Conclusions

This work began by posing the research question: "which of DA-GEE, LR and DA-PLS would be the most effective method for predicting the probability of default?" Further, we asked whether using industry-specific models improves the accuracy of prediction respective to general models.

The methodological comparison has shown that the DA and LR gave nearly the same classification results, thus not permitting identification of one methodology as better than the others (see Table 5.9).

PLS regression gave unsatisfactory results, not so much in terms of the percentage of classification, but in term of the overlapping range of the model Y-predicted. In effect, "getting away" from the default year, the balance-sheet indicators of the two groups of enterprises became too similar and thus any discrimination between them was almost impossible.

Turning to the main research question, it has not been possible to unequivocally prove which is the best applicable methodology, but it is certainly not possible to discard the most innovative: namely, PLS.

Regarding the efficacy of using industry-specific models, the above analyses allow us to accept the original research proposition regarding model generalization, confirming that *specific models improve the accuracy of predictions of default*. This is inferable from the striking reduction in the percentage errors observed in the latter models. This improvement is greater the more homogenous the business conducted by those enterprises. In this, the PLS regression does not differ from traditional methods.

BIBLIOGRAPHY

AA, VV (2000). *I Rating e i Nuovi Strumenti di Controllo Del Rischio di Credito*. Atti convegno 28 settembre 1999 Excelsior Hotel, Il Sole 24Ore, Milano.

AA, VV (2003). Forum su Basilea 2: Quali implicazioni per disponibilità e prezzo del credito? *Economia & Management*, 4, pp. 15–29.

Adam, TR (2002). Risk management and the credit risk premium. *Journal of Banking & Finance*, 26(2–3), pp. 243–269.

Adren, N, H Jankensgard and L Oxelheim (2005). Exposure-based cash-flow-at-risk: An alternative to VAR for industrial companies. *Journal of Applied Corporate Finance*, 17, pp. 76–86.

AIRMIC, ALARM and IRM (2002). A risk management standard. *Institute of Risk Management*, Association of Insurance and Risk Managers.

Alberici, A (1975). *Analisi dei Bilanci e Previsione Delle Insolvenze*. Milan: Isedi.

Alberici, A and S Caselli (2003). *La Valutazione Dell'Impresa Per i Fidi Bancari*. Milan: FrancoAngeli.

Alberici, A and G Forestieri (1986). *La Previsione Delle Insolvenze Bancarie*: *Profili Teorici E Analisi Empiriche*. Milan: Giuffrè.

Alexander, C (1998). *Risk Management and Analysis*: *Measuring and Modeling Financial Risk*. UK: Wiley.

Alici, Y (1996). Neural networks in corporate failure prediction: The UK experience. *Neural Networks in the Capital Market 1995 Proceeding*. Singapore: World Scientific.

Allen, S (2003). *Financial Risk Management*: *A Practitioner's Guide to Managing Market and Credit Risk*. Hoboken: John Wiley & Sons.

Altman, EI (1968). Financial ratios, discriminant analysis and the prediction of corporate bankruptcy. *Journal of Finance*, 23(4), pp. 589–611.

Altman, EI (1984). A further empirical investigation of the bankruptcy cost question. *Journal of Finance*, 39(4), pp. 1067–1089.

Altman, EI (1989). Measuring corporate bond mortality and performances. *Journal of Finance*, 44, pp. 909–922.

Altman, EI (2000). Predicting financial distress of companies: Revisiting the z-score and the zeta models. *Journal of Finance*, 23(4), 589–609.

Altman, EI (2004). Corporate credit scoring insolvency risk models in a benign credit and Basel II environment. New York, NY University Working Paper series.

Altman, EI, RG Haldeman and P Narayanan (1977). Zeta-analysis: A new model to identify bankruptcy risk of corporations. *Journal of Banking and Finance*, 1, pp. 29–54.

Altman, EI, G Marco and F Varetto (1994). Corporate distress diagnosis: Comparisons using linear discriminant analysis and the neural networks (the Italian experience). *Journal of Banking & Finance*, 18, pp. 505–529.

Altman, EI, J Hartzell and M Peck (1995). A Scoring System for Emerging Market Corporate Debt. *Salomon Brothers*, May 15.

Altman, EI and HJ Suggit (2000). Default rates in the syndicated bank loan market: A mortality analysis. *Journal of Banking & Finance*, 24, pp. 229–253.

Altman, EI, G Sabato and N Wilson (2009). The value of qualitative information in SME risk management. *Journal of Credit Risk*, 2, pp. 95–127.

Anmer, J and F Packer (2000). How consistent are credit ratings? A geographic and sectoral analysis of default risk. *International Finance Discussion Papers*, Board of Governors of the Federal Reserve System.

Appetiti, S (1984). *L'utilizzo Dell'analisi Discriminatoria*. Rome: Banca d'Italia.

Archer, Sh and CA D'Ambrosio (1967). *Business Finance: Theory and Management*. New York: Macmillan Publishing.

Arnaboldi, F (2000). Dalla misurazione del rischio dei fidi al credit risk management. *I Rating e i Nuovi Strumenti di Controllo Del Rischio di Credito*. Atti convegno 28 Settembre 1999 Excelsior Hotel, Il Sole 24Ore, Milano.

Arosio, R, G Giudici and S Paleari (2000). What drive the initial market performance of italian IPO's? An empirical investigation on underpricing and price support. Working paper.

Artzner, P, F Delbaen, J Eber and D Heat (1999). Coherent measures of risk. *Mathematical Finance*, 9(3), pp. 203–228.

AS/NZS 4360 (1999). *Risk Management Standards Australia and Standards New Zealand*.

Associazione Bancaria Italiana (2001). *Rischio di Credito, Rating Interni e Cartolarizzazione*. Rome: Edibank.

Associazione Bancaria Italiana (2002). *Loss Given Default: Aspetti Metodologici e Proposta di Una Struttura Dati Per la Stima*. Rome: Bancaria Editrice.

Associazione Bancaria Italiana, Commissione Tecnica Per Gli Studi (1995). *Metodi Avanzati per la Gestione Del Rischio di Credito*. Rome: Bancaria Editrice.

Avesani, R (2000). L'esperienza di Banca Intesa. In Banca d'Italia (ed.), *Modelli per la Gestione Del Rischio di Credito: I Ratings Interni*. Rome: Tematiche Istituzionali.

Ayadi, R and A Resti (2004). *The New Basel Capital Accord and the Future of European Financial System*. Brussels: CEPS.

Aziz, A, DC Emanuel and GH Lawson (1988). Bankruptcy prediction — An investigation of cash flow based models. *Journal of Management Studies*, 25(5), pp. 419–437.

Baden Fuller, C and J Stopford (1994). *Rejuvenating the Mature Business. The Competitive Challenge.* Oxford: Harvard Business School.

Bank of Italy (2000). *Modelli per la Gestione del Rischio di Credito. I Ratings Interni.* Rome: Bank of Italy.

Banks, E (2003). *The Simple Rules of Risk — Revisiting the Art of Financial Risk Management.* Cambridge: Wiley Finance.

Banks, E (2004). *Alternative Risk Transfer Integrated Risk Management through Insurance, Reinsurance, and the Capital Market*, Wiley Finance, Cambridge.

Barnes, P (1982). Methodological implications of non-normality distributed financial ratios. *Journal of Business Finance and Accounting*, 9(1), pp. 51–62.

Baron, DP (1974). Default risk, homemade leverage, and the Modigliani–Miller theorem. *American Economic Review*, 66, pp. 176–182.

Bartram, S (2000). Corporate risk management as a lever for shareholder value creation. *Financial Markets, Institutions and Instruments*, 9(5), pp. 279–325.

Basel Committee (1988). *The Basel Capital Accord.* Basel: Bank for International Settlements.

Basel Committee (2001). *The New Basel Capital Accord.* Basel: Bank for International Settlements.

Basel Committee on Banking Supervision (2003). *The Internal Ratings-Based Approach, Consultative Document.* Basilea: Bank for International Settlements.

Basel Committee on Banking Supervision (2003a). *The New Basel Capital Accord.* Basel: Bank for International Settlements.

Basel Committee on Banking Supervision (2004). *International Convergence of Capital Measurement and Capital Standards: A Revised Framework.* Basilea: Bank for International Settlements.

Basel Committee on Banking Supervision (2004a). *Implementation of the New Capital Adequacy Framework in Non-Basel Committee Member Countries.* Basel: Bank for International Settlements.

Basel Committee on Banking Supervision (2004b). *International Convergence of Capital Measurement and Capital Standards: A Revised Framework.* Basel: Bank for International Settlements.

Beaver, W (1967). Financial ratios predictors of failure. Empirical research in accounting: Selected studies 1966. *Journal of Accounting Research*, 4(Suppl.), pp. 71–111.

Becchetti, L and J Sierra (2002). Bankruptcy risk and productive efficiency in manufacturing firms. *Journal of Banking and Finance*, 27, pp. 2099–2120.

Beretta, S (2004). *Valutazione dei Rischi e Controllo Interno.* Milan: Egea, Università Bocconi Editore.

Berger, AN and GF Udell (1995). Relationship lending and lines of credit in small firm finance. *Journal of Business*, 3, pp. 351–381.

Bertolini, F, F Carniol, G Corvino, G Forestieri, S Paci, L Peccati, F Pichler and R Pisani (2004). *Risk Management, Strumenti e Politiche per la Gestione Dei Rischi Puri Dell'Impresa.* Milan: Etas libri.

Bertoni, A (1996). *Il Rischio di Credito*: *Metodologie Avanzate di Previsione Delle Insolvenze*. Torino: Giappichelli.

Betti, S (2001). *Value at Risk*: *La Gestione Dei Rischi Finanziari e la Creazione Del Valore*. Milan: Il Sole 24Ore.

Bianchi, T (1977). *I Fidi Bancari*: *Tecnica e Valutazione dei Rischi*. Torino: Utet.

Bing, L and R Tiong (1999). Risk management model for international construction joint ventures. *Journal of Construction Engineering and Management*, 125(5), pp. 377–384.

Black, F (1975). Fact and fantasy in the use of options. *Financial Analysts Journal*, July–August, pp. 36–72.

Black, F and JC Cox (1976). Valuing corporate securities: Some effects of bond indenture provisions. *Journal of Finance*, 31(2), pp. 351–367.

Black, F and M Scholes (1973). The pricing of options and corporate liabilities. *Journal of Political Economy*, 81, pp. 637–659.

Blum, M (1974). Failing company discriminant analysis. *Journal of Accounting Research*, 12(1), pp. 1–25.

Boffelli, G (2000). L'assegnazione del rating interno bancario. *Rivista Bancaria Europea*, 15.

Borghesi, A (1985). *La Gestione Dei Rischi di Azienda*. Padova: CEDAM.

Bothers Donald, A (1979). Use of a business failure prediction model for evaluating potential and existing credit risk. *Unpublished M.B.A. Research Project*, Simon Fraser University.

Bozzi, M (2000). Le variabili economiche finanziarie nel processo d'analisi del merito creditizio. In *I Rating e i Nuovi Strumenti di Controllo Del Rischio di Credito*: *Atti Convegno 28 Settembre Excelsior Hotel*. Milano: Il Sole 24Ore.

Brealy, R, S Myers and S Sandri (2003). *Principi di Finanza Aziendale*. Milano: McGraw-Hill.

Brugger, G (1980). *L'Analisi Della Dinamica Finanziaria Dell'Impresa*. Milano: Giuffré.

Callow, D (2005). *Understanding Valuation*: *A Venture Investors Perspect*. San Francisco: Foley & Lardner.

Cameron, IT and R Raman (2005). *Process Systems Risk Management*. The Netherlands: Elsevier.

Cannata, F and S Laviola (2001). *Il Nuovo Accordo Sul Capitale Delle Banche, I Commenti Dell'industria Bancaria, intervento al convegno CERMEF Rischio di credito, nuovo accordo di Basilea e implicazioni per le banche Italiane*. Rome: Banca di Roma.

Cantino, V (2002). *Valore D'impresa e Merito Creditizio*: *Il Rating*. Milano: Giuffrè.

Cantor, R (2001). Moody's investors service response to the consultative paper issued by the Basel Committee on bank supervision: A new capital adequacy framework. *Journal of Banking & Finance*, 25, pp. 171–185.

Cantor, R and F Packer (1995). The credit rating industry. *Journal of Fixed Income*, 5(3), pp. 10–34.

Caprio, L (1999). *Il Capital Assets Pricing Model*, in Cattaneo, M (1999), pp. 275–276.

Carey, M and M Hrycay (2001). Parameterizing credit risk models with rating data. *Journal of Banking & Finance*, 25, pp. 197–270.

Carroll, JM (1984). *Managing Risk*. Boston: Butterworths.

Carty, L (2000). Misurazione del rischio d'inadempienza delle aziende private. In *I Rating e i Nuovi Strumenti di Controllo Del Rischio*, Atti convegno 28 Settembre 1999. Milano: Il Sole 24Ore.

Cattaneo, M (1998). *Finanza Aziendale*. Bologna: Il Mulino.

Cattaneo, M (1999). *Manuale di Finanza Aziendale*. Bologna: Il Mulino.

Cattaneo, M and L Caprio (1999). *Incertezza, Rischio, Comportamento Dell'Investitore*. In Cattaneo, M (ed.), pp. 213–256.

Ceccherelli, A (1931). *Le Prospettive Economiche e Finanziarie Nelle Aziende Commerciali*, Firenze: Barbera.

Ceccherelli, A (1948a). *Economia Aziendale e Amministrazione Delle Imprese*, Firenze: Barbera.

Ceccherelli, A (1948b). *Nozioni di Computisteria, Ragioneria e Pratica Commerciale*, Firenze: Barbera.

Centrale Dei Bilanci (1998) (a cura di). Alberi decisionali e algoritmi genetici nell'analisi del rischio d'insolvenza. *Bancaria*, 1, pp. 74–82.

Chamberlain, G (1983). Funds, factors and diversification in arbitrage pricing models. *Econometrica*, 51, pp. 1301–1324.

Chamberlain, G and M Rothschild (1983). Arbitrage, factor structure, and mean-variance analysis on large asset markets. *Econometrica*, 51, pp. 1281–1304.

Chapman, R (1998). The effectiveness of working group risk identification and assessment. *International Journal of Project Management*, 16(6), pp. 333–343.

Chapman, RJ (2011). *Simple Tools and Techniques for Enterprise Risk Management*. New York: Wiley.

Charitou, A and L Trigeorgis (2002). Option-based bankruptcy prediction. Paper presented at *6th Annual Real Options Conference*, Paphos, Cyprus, 4–6 July, pp. 1–25.

Chen, KH and TA Shimerda (1981). An empirical analysis of useful financial ratio. *Financial Management*, 10(1), pp. 51–60.

Colombi, F (1995). *Baricentro Finanziario*. Rome: Strategie & Finanza.

Comitato di Basilea per la Vigilanza Bancaria (Aprile 2003). *Presentazione Del Nuovo Accordo di Basilea sui Requisiti Patrimoniali*. Basilea: Banca dei Regolamenti Internazionali.

Conti, C (2006). *Introduzione al Corporate Financial Risk Management*. Milan: Pearson.

Coombs, T (1998). An analytic framework for crisis situation: Better responses from a better understanding of the situation. *Journal of Public Relation Research*, 10(3), pp. 177–191.

Cooper Dale, F and R Geoffry (2007). *Project Risk Management Guidelines*, Cambridge: Wiley Finance.

Corsani, G (1937). *La Gestione Delle Imprese Mercantili e Industriali*. Padova: CEDAM.

Corvino, G (1996). Il processo di identificazione del rischio: Descrizione del profilo di rischio e metodologie di ricerca delle informazioni. In Forestieri, G (ed.), *Risk Management. Strumenti e Politiche per la Gestione Dei Rischi Puri Dell'Impresa*. Milano: Egea.

Credit Suisse Financial Products (1997). CreditRisk.

Crouhy, M, D Galai and R Mark (2001). Prototype risk rating system. *Journal of Banking & Finance*, 25, pp. 47–95.

Crouhy, M, D Galai and R Mark (2000). *Risk Management*. New York: McGraw-Hill Companies.

Crowe, R and R Horn (1967). The meaning of risk. *Journal of Risk and Insurance*, 34, pp. 459–474.

Culp, C (2004). *Risk Transfer: Derivatives in Theory and Practice*. Hoboken: John Wiley & Sons.

Cummins, D, R Phillips, R Butsic and R Derring (2000). The risk premium project (RPP). Phase I and II Report, Casualty actuarial Society, Committee on Theory of Risk, June.

Damodaran, A (2006). *Applied Corporate Finance*. New York: Wiley.

Damodaran, A (2011). *Damodaran on Valuation*. New Jersey: Wiley.

Danielis, D (2000). L'esperienza di unicredito Italiano. In Banca d'Italia (ed.), *Modelli Per la Gestione Del Rischio di Credito. I Ratings Interni*. Rome: Tematiche istituzionali.

De Laurentis, G, R Maino and L Molteni (2010). *Developing, Validating and Using Internal Ratings: Methodologies and Case Studies*. UK: Wiley.

De Servigny, A and O Renault (2004). *Measuring and Managing Credit Risk*, McGraw-Hill, New York.

Deakin, E (1972). A discriminant analysis of predictors of business failure. *Journal of Accounting Research*, 10(1), pp. 167–179.

Dell' Amore, G (1965). *Economie delle Aziende di Credito*. Giuffrè: I Prestiti Bancari.

Dickinson, G (2001). Enterprise risk management: Its origins and conceptual foundation. *The Geneva Papers on Risk and Insurance*, 26(3), pp. 360–366.

Diebold, FX, A Bangia, A Kronimus, C Schagen, T Schuermann (2002). Ratings migration and the business cycle, with application to credit portfolio stress testing. *Journal of Banking & Finance*, 26(2–3), pp. 445–474.

Dimson, E, P Marsh and M Staunton (2003). Global evidence on the equity risk premium. *Journal of Applied Corporate Finance*, 15(4), pp. 27–38.

Doherty, NA (1985). *Corporate Risk Management*. New York: McGraw-Hill Book Company.

Duffee, GR (1996). On measuring credit risk of derivatives instruments. *Journal of Banking and Finance*, 20, pp. 805–883.

Ecchia, S (1996). *Il Rischio di Credito. Metodologie Avanzate di Previsione Delle Insolvenze*. Torino: Giappichelli.

Edmister, R (1972). An empirical test of financial ratio analysis for small business failure prediction. *Journal of Financial and Quantitative Analysis*, 7, pp. 1477–1493.

Elton, EJ, MJ Gruber, SJ Brown and WN Goetzmann (2009). *Modern Portfolio Theory and Investment Analysis.* New York: Wiley.

Fanni, M (2000). *Manuale di Finanza Dell'Impresa.* Milan: Giuffrè.

Fazar, W (1959). Program evaluation and review technique. *The American Statistician*, 13(2), p. 10.

Fazzi, R (1940). *Saggio Sui Fondamenti della Teoria Economico-Tecnica del Commercio.* Firenze: Cionini.

Fazzi, R (1942). *Il Trasferimento dei Rischi Aziendali e la Gestione Delle Imprese di Assicurazione.* Firenze: Cionini.

Fazzi, R (1982). *Il Governo Dell'Impresa.* Milan: Giuffré.

Ferrara, F and F Corsi (2006). *L'imprenditore e le società.* Milan: Giuffré.

Ferry, T (1988). *Modern Accident Investigation and Analysis.* New York: Wiley and Sons.

Fink, S (1984). *Crisis Management: Planning for the Inevitable.* New York: Amacom.

Fisher, AR (1936). The use of multiple measurements in taxonomic problems. *Annals of Eugenics*, 7, pp. 179–188.

Fisher, I (1928). *The Money Illusion.* New York: Adelphi.

Fisher, I (1930). The opportunity theory of interest. In Supino, C (ed.), *Economia Politica Contemporanea, Saggi di Economia E Finanza.* Padova: Cedam.

Fisher, I (1930). *The Theory of Interest. As Determined by Impatience to Spend Income and Opportunity to Invest it.* New York: Macmillan Co.

Fitzgerald, AA (1945). Financial and operating ratios. *The Accountant's Journal*, 23(12), pp. 251–256.

Floreani, A (1999). *Altri Modelli di Formazione Del Prezzo Delle Attività Finanziarie.* In Cattaneo, M (ed.), X, pp. 276–305.

Floreani, A (2004). *Enterprise Risk Management. I Rischi Aziendali e Il Processo di Risk Management.* Milan: ISU Università Cattolica.

Floreani, A (2004). *La Valutazione Dei Rischi E Le Decisioni Di Risk Management.* Milan: ISU Università Cattolica.

Floreani, A (2005). *Introduzione al Risk Management: Un Approccio Integrato Alla Gestione Dei Rischi Aziendali.* Milan: Etas Libri.

Forestieri, G (1992). Rischio di credito e finanza d'impresa. *Economia & Management*, 2, pp. 36–42.

Forestieri, G (1996). *Lo Sviluppo Del Risk Management.* In Forestieri, G (ed.). *Condizioni, Limiti, Opportunità Per Le Imprese E Per Il Mondo Assicurativo.* Milan: Egea.

Forestieri, G (a cura di) (1986). *La Previsione Delle Insolvenze Aziendali. Profili Teorici e Analisi Empiriche.* Milan: Giuffrè.

Forestieri, G (a cura di) (1996). *Risk Management. Strumenti e Politiche Per la Gestione Dei Rischi Puri Dell'Impresa.* Milan: Egea.

Forestieri, G and M Onado (a cura di) (1995). *La Gestione del Credito Nelle Banche Europee: Innovazioni Organizzative e Strumenti Per il Controllo del Rischio.* Milan: Egea.

Froot, K and J Stein (1998). Risk management, capital budgeting, and capital structure policy for financial institutions: An integrated approach. *Journal of Financial Economics*, 47(I), pp. 55–82.

Gai, L and F Rossi (2003). Basilea 2: Possibili implicazioni per banche e imprese dall'analisi di un campione di piccole e medie imprese toscane. *Rivista Bancaria*, 2, pp. 23–59.

Generale, A and G Gobbi (1996). *Il Recupero dei Crediti: Costi, Tempi e Comportamenti delle Banche in Temi in Discussione*. Rome: Bank of Italy.

Gentry, JA, P Newbold and DT Whitford (1985). Classifying bankrupt firms with funds flow components. *Journal of Accounting Research*, 23(1), pp. 146–160.

Gifford, S (2010). Risk and uncertainty. In Acs ZJ and Audretsch DB. *International Handbook Series on Entrepreneurship: An Interdisciplinary Survey and Introduction*, pp. 303–318. New York: Springer.

Giunta, F (a cura di) (2002). *Analisi di Bilancio. Teoria e Tecnica*. Firenze: copisteria Il Prato.

Gombola, M, M Haskins, J Ketz and D Williams (1987). Cash flow in bankruptcy prediction. *Financial Management*, 16, pp. 55–65.

Gordon, M (1998). *Production Planning and Controlling*. Illinois: Goodheart-Willcox.

Gordon, MJ and CCY Kwan (1979). Debt maturity, default risk and the capital structure. *Journal of Banking & Finance*, 3, pp. 313–329.

Ghosh, A (2012). *Managing Risks in Commercial and Retail Banking*. Singapore: Wiley.

Grablowski, B and W Talley (1981). Probit and discriminant functions for classifying credit applicants: A comparison. *Journal of Economic and Business*, 33, pp. 254–261.

Grando, A, G Verona and S Vicari (2006). *Tecnologia, Innovazione e Operations*. Milan: Egea.

Green, MR and ORN Serbein (1983). *Risk Management: Text and Cases*. Reston: Reston Publishing.

Greene, M and O Serbein (1983). *Risk Management. Text and Cases*. Reston: Reston Publishing.

Griep, C and M De Stefano (2001). Standard & Poor's official response to the Basel committee's proposal. *Journal of Banking & Finance*, 25, pp. 149–169.

Griffin, H and M Dugan (2003). Systematic risk and revenue volatility. *Journal of Financial Research*, 26(2), pp. 179–189.

Guatri, L and M Bini (1998). *Trattato Sulla Valutazione Delle Imprese*. Milan: Egea.

Hampton, JJ (2009). *Fundamentals of Enterprise Risk Management: How Top Companies Assess Risk, Manage Exposures, and Seize Opportunities*. New York: Amacon.

Hull, JC (2003). *Opzioni, Futures e Altri Derivati*. Milan: Il Sole 24Ore.

Hull, JC (2006). *Options, Futures and other Derivatives* (6th edn.). Upper Saddle River, New Jersey: Pearson Prentice Hall.

Hull, JC (2012). *Risk Management and Financial Institutions*. New Jersey: Wiley.

Iben, T and R Litterman (1989). Corporate bond valuation and the term structure of credit spreads. *Journal of Portfolio Management*, Spring, pp. 52–64.

Ingersoll, J (1984). Some results in the theory of arbitrage pricing. *Journal of Finance*, 39, pp. 1021–1039.

Jacobson, T and K Roszbach (2003). Bank lending policy, credit scoring and value at risk. *Journal of Banking & Finance*, 27(4), pp. 615–633.

Jensen, MC (1986). Agency costs of free cash flow, corporate finance and takeovers. *American Economic Review*, 76, pp. 323–329.

Jonkhart, M (1979). On the term structure of interest rates and the risk of default. *Journal of Banking and Finance*, 3(3), pp. 253–262.

Kahneman, D, P Slovic and A Tversky (1982). *Judgement under Uncertainty: Heuristics and Biases*. Cambridge: Cambridge University Press.

Karels, GV and AJ Prakash (1987). Multivariate normality and forecasting of business bankruptcy. *Journal of Business Finance & Accounting*, 14(4), pp. 573–593.

Keasey, K and R Watson (1991). Financial distress models: A review of their usefulness. *British Journal of Management*, 2(2), pp. 89–102.

Keynes (1930). *The General Theory of Employment, Interest and Money*. London: MacMillan.

Klugman, S, H Panjer and G Willmot (1998). *Loss Models: From Data to Decisions*. Hoboken (NJ): John Wiley & Sons.

Kmv Corporation (1994). *Credit Monitoring*. San Francisco: Kmv Corporation.

Knight, FH (1921). *Risk, Uncertainty, and Profit*. Hart, Schaffner, and Marx Prize Essays, No. 31. Boston and New York: Houghton Mifflin.

Koller, G (1999). *Risk Assessment and Decision Making in Business and Industry: A Practical Guide*. Boca Raton: CRC Press LLC.

Krahnen, JP and M Weber (2001). Generally accepted rating principles: A primer. *Journal of Banking & Finance*, 25, pp. 3–23.

Kraus, F and A Litzenberg (1973). A state preference model of optimal financial leverage. *Journal of Finance*, 28, pp. 911–922.

La Sacra Bibbia, Genesi, 3, pp. 23–24.

Laitinen, E and T Laitinen (2000). Bankruptcy prediction: Application of the Taylor's expansion in logistic regression. *International Review of Financial Analysis*, 9, pp. 239–269.

Lando, D (2004). *Credit Risk Modeling*. New Jersey: Princeton University Press.

Lando, D and TM Skodeberg (2002). Analyzing rating transitions and rating drift with continuos observations. *Journal of Banking & Finance*, 26(2–3), pp. 423–444.

Lenoci, F and S Peola (2004), *Negoziare Con le Banche Alla Luce di Basilea 2, I Cambiamenti Per le Imprese e le Banche*. Milan: IPSOA.

Liebenberg, A and R Hoyt (2003). The determinants of enterprise risk management: Evidence from the appointment of chief risk officer. *Risk Management and Insurance Review*, 6(1), pp. 37–52.

Lintner, J (1965a). Security prices, risk, and maximal gains from diversification. *Journal of Finance*, 20, pp. 587–615.

Lintner, J (1965b). The valuation of risk assets and the selection of risky investments in stock portfolios and capital budgets. *Review of Economics and Statistics*, 47(1), pp. 13–37.

Lo, AW (1986). Logit versus discriminant analysis: A specification test and application to corporate bankruptcies. *Journal of Econometrics*, 31(2), pp. 151–178.

Luerti, A (1992). *La Previsione Dello Stato D'Insolvenza Delle Imprese. Il Modello AL/93*. Milano: Etaslibri.

Lussier, RN (1995). A non-financial business success versus failure prediction model for young firms. *Journal of Small Business Management*, 33(1), pp. 8–20.

Macminn, RD (2002). Value at risk: A comment. *Journal of Banking & Finance*, 26(2–3), pp. 297–301.

Malcolm, DG, JH Roseboom, CE Clark and W Fazar (1959). Application of a technique for research and development program evaluation. *Operations Research*, 7(5), pp. 646–669.

Mandelker, G and S Rhee (1984). The impact of the degrees of operating and financial leverage on systematic risk of common stock. *Journal of Financial and Quantitative Analysis*, 19, pp. 45–57.

Martin, D (1977). Early warning of bank failures: A logit regression approach. *Journal of Banking & Finance*, 1, pp. 249–276.

Martin, J and A Sayrak (2003). Corporate diversification and shareholder value: A survey of recent literature. *Journal of Corporate Finance*, 9, pp. 37–57.

McAllister, PH and JJ Mingo (1994). Commercial loan risk management, credit-scoring, and pricing: The need for a new shared database. *The Journal of Commercial Lending*, 76(9), pp. 6–22.

Mc Leay, S and A Omar (2000). The sensitivity of prediction models to the non-normality of bounded and unbounded financial ratios. *British Accounting Review*, 32, pp. 213–230.

Merna, T and FF Al-Thani (2011). *Corporate Risk Management*. UK: Wiley.

Merton, R (1973). The rational theory of options pricing. *The Bell Journal of Economics and Management Science*, 4, pp. 141–183.

Merton, RC (1974). On the pricing of corporate debt: The risk structure of interest rate. *Journal of Finance*. 1(5–6), pp. 6–22.

Meulbroek, L (2002). Integrated risk management for the firm: A senior's managers guide. *Journal of Applied Corporate Finance*, 14, pp. 56–70.

Miccolis, J and S Shah (2000). *Enterprise Risk Management: An Analytic Approach*. New York: Tillinghast-Towers Perrin.

Micha, B (1984). Analysis of business failures in France. *Journal of Banking and Finance*, 8, pp. 281–291.

Miles, JA and JR Ezzel (1980). The weighted average cost of capital, perfect capital markets and project life: A clarification. *Journal of Financial and Quantitative Analysis*, 15.

Mill, JS (1848). *Principles of Political Economy with Some of Their Applications to Social Philosophy*. London: Parker.

Miller, M (1977). Debt and taxes. *Journal of Finance*, 32, 261–275.

Minty, G (1998). *Production Planning and Controlling*. US: Goodheart–Willcox.

Misani, N (1999). *Il Risk Management Fra Assicurazione e Finanza. Nuove Tecniche di Gestione Dei Rischi Puri*: Catastrophe Bonds, Derivati Assicurativi, Capitale Contingente, Risk Fusion. Milan: Egea.

Modigliani, F and M Miller (1958). The cost of capital, corporation finance and the theory of investment. *The American Economic Review*, 48(3), pp. 261–297.

Modigliani, F and M Miller (1963). Corporate income taxes and the cost of capital: A correction. *The American Economic Review*, 53(3), pp. 433–443.

Monahan, G (2008). *Enterprise Risk Management: A Methodology for Achieving Strategic Objectives*. New Jersey: Wiley.

Moody's Investor Service (1991). *Global Credit Analysis*. London: IFR Publishing.

Morgan, JP (1997). *CreditMetrics*. New York: J.P. Morgan & Co.

Mossman, CE, GG Bell, LM Swartz and H Turtle (1998). An empirical comparison of bankruptcy models. *The Financial Review*, 33(2), pp. 35–54.

Murphy, D (2008). *Understanding Risk: The Theory and Practice of Financial Risk Management*. USA: Chapman & Hall.

Myers, S (1968). Procedures for capital budgeting under uncertainty. *Industrial Management Review*, 9 (Spring), pp. 1–20.

Myers, S (1974). Interactions of corporate financing and investment decisions-implications for capital budgeting. *Journal of Finance*, 29, pp. 1–25.

Myers, SC (1984). The capital structure puzzle. *Journal of Finance*, 39, pp. 575–592.

Nocco, BW and RM Stulz (2006). Enterprise risk management: Theory and practice. *Journal of Applied Corporate Finance*, 18(4), pp. 8–20.

Ohlson, J (1980). Financial ratios and the probabilistic prediction of bankruptcy. *Journal of Accounting Research*, 18(1), pp. 109–131.

Olson, DL and D Wu Dash (2008). *Enterprise Risk Management*. Singapore: World Scientific Publishing Co Pte Ltd.

Ong, MK (1999). *Internal Credit Risk Models: Capital Allocation and Performance Measurement*. London: Risk Books.

Ooghe, H, P Joos and C De Bourdeaudhuij (1995). Financial distress models in Belgium: The results of a decade of empirical research. *The International Journal of Accounting*, 30, pp. 245–274.

Pennock, M and Y Haimes (2002). Principles and guidelines for project risk management. *System Engineering*, 5(2), pp. 89–108.

Perold, A (2001). Capital Allocation in Financial Firms, Competition and Strategy. *Working Paper Series*, Harvard Business School, 98, p. 72.

Pivato, S (1983). *Trattato di Finanza Aziendale*. Milan: FrancoAngeli.

Pivato, S (1992). La protezione delle risorse aziendali. In Guatri, L (ed.), *Economia Delle Aziende Industriali e Commerciali*. Milan: Egea.

Platt, HD and MB Platt (1990). Development of a class of stable predictive variables: the case of bankruptcy prediction. *Journal of Business Finance & Accounting*, 17(1), pp. 31–51.

Porter, ME (1980). *La Strategia Competitiva. Analisi per le Decisioni*. Bologna: Edizioni della tipografia dei compositori.

Porter, ME (1987). *Il Vantaggio Competitivo*. Milan. Edizioni di Comunità.

PricewaterhouseCoopers (1996). *Enhancing Shareholder Wealth by Better Managing Business Risk*. New York: International Federation of Accountants.

Rappaport, A (1986). *Creating Shareholder Value: The New Standard for Business Performance*. New York: Free Press.

Reilly, AH (1987). Are organizations ready for crises? A managerial Scorecard. *Columbia Journal of World Business*, 22, pp. 79–88.

Renn, O (1998). Three decades of risk research: Accomplishments and new challenges. *Journal of Risk Research*, 1(1), pp. 49–71.

Resti, A (2002). La riforma dei requisiti patrimoniali obbligatori: Effetti sulla qualità dell'offerta di credito. In Masciandaro, D and G Bracchi (eds.), *La banca, leregole e l'etica: stabilità integrità e sostenibilità*. Rome: Fondazione Rosselli, Edibank.

Resti, A and A Sironi (2007). *Risk Management and Shareholders' Value in Banking: From Risk Measurement Models to Capital Allocation Policies*. UK: Wiley.

Reuvid, J (2005). *Managing Business Risk — A Practical Guide to Protecting Your Business* (2nd edn.). London: Kogan Page.

Ricardo, D (1817). *On the Principles of Political Economy and Taxation*. London: John Murray, Chapters 1 and 5.

Riparbelli, A (1950). *Il Contributo Della Ragioneria All'Analisi Dei Dissesti*. Firenze: Stabilimenti Grafici Vallechi, p. 73.

Roggi, O (2003). *Valore Intrinseco e Prezzo di Market nelle Operazioni di Finanza Straordinaria*. Milan: Franco Angeli.

Roggi, O (2007). Basel II e default risk estimation. Conference Proceedings *Small business banking and financing: S global perspective*, Cagliari.

Roggi, O (2009). *Rischio, Valore e Insolvenza*. Milan: FrancoAngeli.

Roll, R (1977). An analytical formula for unprotected American call options on stocks with known dividends. *Journal of Financial Economics*, 5, pp. 251–258.

Ross, S (1976). The arbitrage theory of capital asset pricing. *Journal of Economic Theory*, 13(3), pp. 341–360.

Runde, J (1998). Clarifying Frank Knight's discussion of the meaning of risk and uncertainty. *Cambridge Journal of Economics*, 22, pp. 539–546.

Saita, F (2007). *Value at Risk and Bank Capital Management*. USA: Elsevier.

Saunders, A (1997). *Financial Institutions Management*. Boston: Irwin Publishing.

Saunders, A and EI Altman (2001). An analysis and critique of the BIS proposal on capital adequacy and ratings. *Journal of Banking & Finance*, 25, pp. 25–46.

Saunders, A and L Allen (2002). *Credit Risk Measurement: New Approaches to Value at Risk and Other Paradigms*. New York: Wiley.

Scarelandi, P (2000). L'esperienza di San Paolo IMI. In Banca d'Italia, *Modelli per la Gestione del Rischio di Credito. I Ratings Interni*. Roma: Tematiche Istituzionali.

Schall, LD and GL Sundem (1980). Capital budgeting methods and risk. *Financial Management*, 9, pp. 161–179.

Schroeck, G (2002). *Risk Management and Value Creation in Financial Institutions*. New Jersey: Wiley.

Schumpeter, JA (1948). Irving Fisher's econometrics. *Econometrica*, 3, July, pp. 219–231.

Shall, L (1972). Asset valuation, firm investment and firm diversification. *Journal of Business*, pp. 11–28.

Sharpe, W (1964). Capital asset prices: A theory of market equilibrium under condition of risk. *Journal of Finance*, 19, pp. 425–442.

Shimpi, P (2001). *Integrated Corporate Risk Management*. New York: Texere.

Sierra, J and L Becchetti (2003). Bankruptcy risk and productive efficiency in manufacturing firms. *Journal of Banking & Finance*, 27(11), pp. 2099–2120.

Sironi, A (2000). La misurazione e la gestione del rischio di credito: Approcci alternativi, obiettivi e applicazioni. In Savona, P and A Sironi (eds.), *La Gestione del Rischio di Credito, Esperienze e Modelli nelle Grandi Banche Italiane*. Italy: Edibank.

Sironi, A (2005). *Rischio e Valore Nelle Banche*. Milan: Egea.

Sironi, A and P Savona (a cura di) (2000). *La Gestione Del Rischio di Credito: Esperienze e Modelli Nelle Grandi Banche Italiane*. Roma: Edibank.

Smith, CW (1980). On the theory of financial contracting: The personal loan market. *Journal of Monetary Economics*, 6, pp. 333–357.

Smith, CW, CW Smithson and DS Wilford (1990). *Managing Financial Risk*. New York: Harper Business.

Smith D (a cura di) (2002). *Business Continuity Management: Good Practice Guidelines*. UK: Business Continuity Institute.

Smith, J (2003). The shareholder vs. stakeholder debate. *MIT Sloan Management Review*, 44, Summer, pp. 85–90.

Smithson, C (2003). *Credit Portfolio Management*. New Jersey: Wiley.

Springate, Gordon LV (1978). Predicting the possibility of failure in a Canadian firm. *Unpublished M.B.A. Research Project*, Simon Fraser University, January.

Standard & Poor's (1996). *Corporate Rating Criteria*. New York: Standard & Poor's.

Standard & Poor's (1998). *Ratings performance 1997: Stability and Transition*. New York: Standard & Poor's.

Standard & Poor's (2002). *Credit Risk Tracker Italy*. Technical document.

Stein, J, S Usher, D LaGatutta and J Youngen (2001). A comparables approach to measuring cash flow-at-risk for non-financial firms. *Journal of Applied Corporate Finance*, 13(4), pp. 100–109.

Stevenson, WJ (1996). *Production-Operations Management* (5th edn.). Boston: McGraw-Hill.

Stewart, B (1991). *Eva. The Quest for Value*. New York: Harper Business.

Taffler, RJ and H Tisshaw (1977). Going, going, gone — four factors which predict. *Accountancy*, 88, pp. 50–54.

Terriero (ABI) (2003). Nuovi approcci nella valutazione del rischio di credito delle imprese: Sistemi di internal rating. Atti convegno, Brescia, 21 gennaio 2003.

Tenenhaus, M (1995). A partial least squares approach to multiple regression, redundancy analysis and canonical analysis. *Les Cahiers de Recherche de HEC*, CR 550/1995.

Tenenhaus, M and VE Vinzi (2005). PLS regression, PLS path modeling and generalized Procrustean analysis: A combined approach for multiblock analysis. *Journal of Chemometrics*, 19(3), pp. 145–153.

Tobin, J (1985). Neoclassical theory in America: JB Clark and Fisher. *American Economic Review*, 75(6), pp. 28–38.

Treynor, J (1961). Market value, time and risk. *Unpublished document*.

Trippi, RR and W Turban (1993). *Neural Networks in Finance and Investing*. Chicago: Irwin Publishing.

Van Gestel, T and B Baesens (2009). *Credit Risk Management: Basic Concepts, Financial Risk Components, Rating Analysis, Models, Economic and Regulatory Capital*. Oxford: Oxford University Press.

Varetto, F (1990). *Il Sistema di Diagnosi Dei Rischi di Insolvenza Delle Centrale Bilanci*. Roma: Bancaria Editrice.

Varetto, F and G Marco (1994). *Diagnosi Dell'insolvenza Aziendale Con Reti Neurali*. Roma: Bancaria Editrice.

Vinzi, VE, CN Lauro and S Amato (2002). PLS typological regression: Algorithmic, classification and validation issues. In *New Developments in Classification and Data Analysis*, pp. 133–140. Heidelberg: Springer.

Vose, D (2000). *Risk Analysis: A Quantitative Guide*. Chichester, West Sussex: John Wiley & Sons.

Walras, L (1874). *Elements D'Economie Politique Pure*. Paris: Economia.

Wiginton, J (1980). A note on the comparison of logit and discriminant models of consumer credit behaviour. *Journal of Financial and Quantitative Analysis*, 5, pp. 757–770.

Willet, HA (1901). *The Economic Theory of Risk and Insurance*. New York: The Columbia University Press.

Wilson, RL and R Sharda (1993). Bankruptcy prediction using neural networks. In Trippi, RR and E Turban (eds.). *Neural Networks in Finance and Investing*. Chicago: Irwin Publishing.

Wilson, T (1997a). Portfolio credit risk (I). *Risk*, 10(9), pp. 111–117.

Wilson, T (1997b). Portfolio credit risk (II). *Risk*, 10(10), pp. 56–61.

Yang, ZR, H James and A Packer (1997). *The Failure Prediction of UK Private Construction Companies*. UK: Mimeo.

Zappa, G (1927). *Tendenze Nuove Negli Studi Di Ragioneria*. Milan: Istituto Editoriale Scientifico.

Zavgren, C (1983). The prediction of corporate failure: The state of the art. *Journal of Accounting Literature*, 2, pp. 1–37.

Zazzara, C (2001). I modelli per il rischio di credito nel nuovo accordo di Basilea", relazione presentata al convegno Cermef, *Rischio di credito, nuovo accordo di Basilea e implicazioni per le banche italiane*, Banca di Roma, Roma.

Zmiewski, M and B Foster (1996). Credit scoring speeds small business loan processing. *Journal of Lending & Credit Risk Management*, 79(3), pp. 42–47.

Zmijewski, ME (1984). Methodological issues related to the estimation of financial distress prediction models. *Journal of Accounting Research*, 22, pp. 59–86.

INDEX

Printed in the United States
By Bookmasters